A MOTHER'S

A Mother's Instincts

THE EXTRAORDINARY INTUITIONS
OF ORDINARY WOMEN

Cassandra Eason

Aquarian/Thorsons
An Imprint of HarperCollinsPublishers

The Aquarian Press
An Imprint of HarperCollins*Publishers*
77–85 Fulham Palace Road,
Hammersmith, London W6 8JB

Published by The Aquarian Press 1992
1 3 5 7 9 10 8 6 4 2

A catalogue record for this book
is available from the British Library

ISBN 1 85538 124 9

Typeset by Harper Phototypesetters Limited,
Northampton, England
Printed in Great Britain by
HarperCollins Manufacturing Glasgow

CONTENTS

CONTENTS

1

In Search of the Psychic Link

Annette was enjoying a rare evening at the cinema with her husband when an inexplicable sense of danger made her rush home to save her baby's life. At the time she and her husband were employed as cook and waiter respectively in a hotel in Surrey, and lived along with their six-month-old daughter in a little cottage near the hotel. 'We could only rarely go out together, as we each had different days off, ' she said. 'But on this rare occasion we both got an evening off together, so we went to see a film in the nearest town, about six miles away. One of the hotel staff had volunteered to babysit, and we set off to catch a bus.

'We had not been in the cinema for more than a few minutes when a terrible uneasiness came over me. I could distinctly smell something burning. I fidgeted a lot and my husband asked what was wrong. I told him I could smell burning. He said I'd probably dropped a bit of my cigarette. I stooped and had a look on the carpet but there was no sign of any glowing ash. The smell persisted, and eventually I told my husband I was leaving. He followed me reluctantly, muttering something derogatory about women.

'As we boarded the bus for home I prayed for it to go faster. At last we were sprinting down the lane leading to the cottage. The smell of burning was now very definite, though my husband still could not smell anything. We reached the door, which I literally burst through. As I did dense smoke poured out, and a chair by the fire burst into flames. I rushed through to the bedroom and got the baby out while my husband dragged out the unconscious babysitter. She had fallen asleep and dropped her lighted cigarette onto the chair.'

This incident happened in 1936. The baby is now grown up and is living in the United States, the mother of six children. The phenomenon remains as inexplicable now as it was then.

Annette's own explanation, recorded in the archives of the Alister Hardy Research Centre for Religious and Spiritual Experience in Oxford, is: 'I believe God sent me home to save my baby.' The religiously inclined may see the hand of God in such events, but for others it can be put under the heading of maternal instinct.

This instinct, which seems to encompass the fields labelled telepathy, premonition, second sight or just plain woman's intuition, yet is somehow stronger and more wide-reaching than all these, is not one rooted in logic nor open to scientific measurement. Countless women throughout the world have heard its call, and by acting upon it have averted potential disaster. While some see it as a religious experience, for others it is rooted in their physical as well as mental and spiritual closeness with a child who was once part of their body. Such views need not be conflicting, and arguments over terminology simply obscure the essence of the experience. Sceptics will say it is all in a woman's mind, but it works. Women use it not only as dramatically as Annette did but also in the everyday interactions of mother and child. In any terms, what happens between mother and child is pretty special.

Just how it works is difficult to define, because the warnings arrive in so many different ways. For Annette, her instinct appeared to act through her sense of smell to alert her to her child's danger. But for another mother in a very similar situation the warning signal was visual.

David Crawford, who now lives in the Haute Savoie region of France, told me that when he was five and living in Scotland he went to the dentist to have a tooth removed. 'The dentist had considerable difficulty stemming the flow of blood. Everything had been sorted out by the evening, however, and my parents had gone out to the local cinema while I was left with a babysitter. I had fallen asleep and the babysitter was downstairs, having checked on me in bed.

'During the middle of the film my mother saw before her a vision of my face covered in blood rather than the picture the rest of the audience was seeing. She persuaded my father that something was wrong with me and that they must return home immediately. Reluctantly my father agreed. They arrived home and my mother rushed upstairs to my bedroom, to find that my gums had started to bleed again profusely and that, as I was lying on my back, the blood had started to run back up my nose and I was at the point of asphyxiation.'

Many parents have told me of this psychic link with their children. The incidents are usually related by women. Perhaps because they carry the growing child for nine months in their bodies, or because even today childcare largely falls upon the mother or mother substitute, so that in practical terms the mother and the child are closest physically and mentally.

But although the phenomenon is common knowledge among mothers, it is rarely discussed. Many mothers are reluctant to talk about what cannot be explained in straightforward terms, and fear they will be labelled 'hormonal'.

I would not have talked about it, much less written about it, had I not been catapulted into it by a sixth-sense link, not with me, but between my middle son and his father. Dads can and do have this instinct, but it's very hard for them to acknowledge it in a society where many women still want a macho man though they may on the surface berate the poor guy because he is not more caring. My third son had been held and cared for at birth by his father, John, since I was recovering from an emergency Caesarean. Indeed, John had caused great amusement and admiration in the maternity ward by popping in to change the baby's nappy. Because he worked irregular hours as a freelance journalist, he was around during the day to take an active part in the routine work of childcare. Perhaps as a result of this close contact the baby would always wake five minutes before his dad came home, even though, because of the nature of his work, there was no regular pattern night or day to John's return.

One morning when John had been on an overnight shift my son, then two-and-a-half, announced quite calmly that daddy had gone roly-poly on his motor bike but was all right. At that moment, forty miles away on the approach to the M4 motorway out of London, my husband's motor bike was skidding on a patch of oil and he was sliding along the tarmac. Fortunately, as my mini-prophet had told me, dad was a bit battered but unbowed. John wrote an article in *The Guardian* about the incident, I think half in the hope that someone might come up to him and explain it away. As I said, men are not always entirely comfortable with these unexplained phenomena flying around. He got very little response, apart from one or two dads who admitted at the pub that they'd had similar experiences.

In contrast I got an overwhelming response from mothers at the playgroup, in the park and in the playground. They said that similar things had happened with their children and that they would tell me if I promised not to reveal their names. The subject of everyday extrasensory communication is still quite taboo, especially in Britain. Indeed, on a recent radio phone-in I was talking about maternal intuition when a woman listener, a trainee psychiatrist, suggested I shouldn't be dabbling in black magic but should encourage women to tell psychologists about their problems. My first book, *The Psychic Power of Children* (Rider, 1990), told of many inexplicable incidents involving children. But an intriguing thread ran through it that I felt deserved further investigation. Many of the experiences I discovered were rooted in the young child's ability to know the unknowable and make no big deal of it. But equally, some experiences I came across didn't come from a child but from his or her mother, who had responded to her child's unspoken distress signal, perhaps from many miles away. Where the child was apparently in possession of telepathic powers, it was usually the mother's mind the child was reading. 'I can see the pictures in your mind,' said five-year-old Dom to his mother Cathy, and the jigsaw started to fall into place.

The magic was inherent in the bond between child and mother, a bond that began well before birth and in some cases survived even death. And many unexplained maternal-child events in my own family fitted into the jigsaw. I wished someone had told me as a new mother that the solution that came naturally from within was usually the best – that I, as a mother, was the expert on the child who had sprung from my body. I have five children, the youngest of whom is only three. With my first two infants I relied entirely on conventional methods of communication and interaction. I read the right books and attended classes on every imaginable aspect of physical, mental and spiritual child-rearing. Advice came by the encyclopaedia-load from paediatricians and relatives. Even the caretaker at the school I taught at during my first pregnancy added his piece. If I stood on a chair to hang pictures on the classroom wall I would strangle my unborn child with his umbilical cord. This helpful advice was matched only by the tale I recently heard from the US about the dangers of new mothers playing tennis in the sun: apparently their breast-milk turns to butter!

Throughout the babyhood and early childhood of my first two children I acted as glorified cheer-leader, making sure their every waking moment was filled with stimulating and socially-adjusted activity. Living by the book? I tried to live by them all, the whole pile of them. I frantically rifled through them at every crisis. Have you every tried to adjust an infant's four-meals-a-day weaning schedule to allow for the change to British Summer Time?

Was it worth it? When my first born had to be dragged into nursery school by his feet screaming blue murder, I howled almost as loudly as he did. I had totally failed to live up to the perfect, smiling mother-image I had created for myself from the Lego-land of calm, all-embracing maternal models from the Virgin Mary to the gleaming mums on telly soap-powder advertisements.

By my third child I was so tired that I simply gave up trying to be super-mum – and everything fell into place. If the baby cried I cuddled him, if he was hungry I fed him. If I was fed up I told him so, and if he didn't want to play with the children down the road, so what? It was brilliant, and by child number four the family was backpacking to Paris. My younger three children are as just socially and intellectually advanced as their elders in spite of my apparent maternal neglect, and have an additional ease with the world and a cheerful acceptance as well as an amazing adaptability when things do go wrong.

But the most exciting product of my new acceptance of my own and my children's imperfections was that quite automatically I knew what to do in a crisis. I could anticipate when the children would wake, even when there was an imminent mood-change and potential tantrum. Most strangely, when I was absent from the children I knew times that they needed me. Once I stopped consciously monitoring, some deeper level of 'automatic pilot' took over which was much more accurate and sensitive, a sort of psychic early warning system of hazards round the corner. Of course it wasn't as specific as that, and didn't always work. But it is nevertheless the most under-utilized 'mother's help'.

Let's look at a common experience. Anne Burbidge of Leicester was slogging through the snow when the message came to her: drop everything and run. 'My fifth child was born at the beginning of November, 1986. A few days before my husband's birthday in January we had a great deal of snow. It was impossible to drive, push a pram or take a baby out in a carrier. I needed to buy a present for my husband, so reluctantly I left the baby with my mother. Once I got to the main road I managed to catch a bus, and I was soon enjoying browsing round the shops on my own – something I had not done for some time. Suddenly I had the feeling that I had to go home. I just turned and left the shop I was in without buying anything and began hurrying home as fast as I could, without even waiting for the bus. I felt in quite a panic – hurrying uphill through the thick snow every step seemed to take an eternity.

'I found my mother just about managing to pacify a baby who was ready for a feed. She told me the little one had started to stir about twenty minutes before, just about the time when I had felt the overwhelming urge to hurry home.'

It could be argued that it was normal for Anne to be anxious about leaving a small child for the first time, and that her return home to find the baby crying was a coincidence. But Anne was not a first-time mother; she had four other children. Nor was she anxious when the distress signal came to her. And the call, as any mother who has experienced it will know, is very different from ordinary, run-of-the-mill maternal anxiety. Someone described it as the feeling you get when you have had too much coffee: the jitters. It can be physically felt as an urgent stabbing in the gut, or heard as a voice saying 'Go home now.'

That the psychic link is not one of 'normal anxiety' is demonstrated by my own experiences. The first time I left my first child should have been the time I heard the call. I was all primed up for it. My pure relief to be away for a while was tinged with guilt that I was deserting my post. But for two hours I walked around an East London shopping mall totally unaware that my baby was yelling his head off the entire time. Maybe I would have known if I had listened to my inner voice instead of worrying and rationalizing my feelings. With my youngest child I am happier to acknowledge the link I can't explain scientifically, and so I can use it. Quantum potential, the latest attempt to explain telepathy scientifically, doesn't really seem to cover the feeling – something akin to labour pains – which had me dashing home ten miles from the supermarket as my youngest was being fished out of the river – unhurt but screaming his head off.

I have collected experiences from women all round the world telling how this instinct has helped them, in the hope that this book will give other women the confidence to follow their own intuitions in mothering. Many mother-and-baby organizations and breast-feeding leagues have granted me access to their members, and in many cases it is the leaders of the groups who have sent me their personal insights. The organizations that I know personally to be both sympathetic and of practical use to mothers are listed in the Helpful Addresses section at the back of the book. In no way am I claiming association with any of the mother-baby leagues or reflecting their philosophies. This is essentially a book about and for individual woman world-wide who have felt the pull of a mother's instincts and who want other women to know they are not alone and can trust the greatest gift in every woman, her sixth sense, intuition, a magical bond, whatever we choose to call it.

The maternal intuitive link is naturally strongest when your children are young. It can, however, be a valuable tool during the more turbulent adolescent years, when conventional parent-child contact can be at a minimum. Indeed, this instinct can last into your children's adult years, and many women still routinely communicate with their own mothers telepathically. How often do they try to phone each other only to get the engaged tone, and when they do speak both say at once: 'But I was trying to call you.'?

Although this is most common between mother and daughter it also occurs, albeit less frequently, between mother and son. Enid, who lives in the south of England, can tell when her 30-year-old son is going to ring her even though he is a sailor and sometimes cannot find a telephone or get a shore line from one week to the next. She will suddenly say to her husband: 'We can't go out; David is going to ring.' Five minutes later there is a phone call from David in the Falklands or Fiji. This doesn't surprise Enid at all: 'Why shouldn't I know?' she says, 'David and I have always been close, from when he was a baby.'

For many parents this bond is especially activated by distress in the adult fledgling. When David was based in Portsmouth and Enid living some 70 miles away she could not settle one evening for worrying about him for no apparent reason. She knew he would not be home from the naval base then so she didn't ring. Then at nine o'clock she felt so ill she told her husband she had to go to bed. At that moment her son was walking through his door to discover a goodbye note left him by his wife. She had walked out for good at about the time Enid had started to feel uneasy.

As I have said, the magical communication between mother and child does not occur at times of crisis alone. It can be an unspoken part of everyday family life, as Wendy Hutton from Hampshire relates. 'I was washing my hair and thinking I hadn't seen my old friend Julie for some time. Within seconds four-year-old Jo piped up, "When are we going to see Aunty Julie again, Mummy?". Julie had not been mentioned in conversation for some months, and there was no reason why Jo should ask the question unless she was picking something up from me telepathically.'

The difference between the type of experience Wendy describes and the more conventional view of childhood psychic experiences is that here the parental link triggers psychic ability. The information the child transmits is not random nor concerned with global events but rather comes from the mother's psyche. The child is less likely to read the mind of the woman at the bus stop, though maybe he could if he chose, because it is the love and caring between mother and child that is the driving force behind these instinctual experiences.

The maternal/child sixth sense connection is not a purely genetic one, either. This information may be disappointing for those who anticipate that one day we shall be able explain away the magical link in terms of DNA strands, if the quantum potentialists don't get there first. Close, intuitive bonds are often found between children and their foster and adoptive parents. Rita Laws, of Oklahoma in the US, a researcher into the maternal psychic bond who has seven adopted children as well as three birthchildren, found that the psychic link between her and her birthson Joaquin was not only equally effective but also equally painful to that with her adopted son Jesse. When Joaquin and Jesse were four and three-and-a-half years old she developed a toothache in her left lower middle molar. 'The tooth looked fine but it hurt a lot. After about a week of this it stopped. Then the same tooth directly across on the other side began hurting too. After that stopped, both molars began to hurt very badly at the same time. The dentist could find nothing wrong and sent me to a specialist. The specialist examined my teeth and took some X-rays, but also found absolutely nothing wrong. I went home discouraged and confused.

'The next morning the toothaches were gone and I was thrilled. But after breakfast Joaquin complained of a toothache. When I looked in his mouth I was horrified to see the lower molar on the left side was half eaten away with decay. The tooth was all but lost. Then Jesse mentioned that his tooth had been hurting, too. I looked in his mouth and saw the lower molar on the right side in the same horrid condition! Both boys had to have crowns put on those bad teeth, but after that was done I never experienced the phantom toothache again. And I now supervise tooth-brushing more carefully.'

How then do these instincts work? If science cannot provide an answer then perhaps all we can do is try to identify the common strand that seems to run through all these experiences whether the women interpret the moving force as something divine or as a contact with some inner perhaps equally universal force. Deep love and acceptance between mother and child is present in every experience I researched, although that is not to say there are no doubts or negative feelings too. I am writing about real women, not plaster saints or the women from the adverts. The love they feel is not sentimental or sickly but holds mother and child together, sometimes only by the finest thread, no matter what is happening.

Rather than asking how these instincts work we should perhaps ask what are their purpose, and how can they be used. For this is not just a book of amazing stories but an attempt to come to grips with this mysterious and unpredictable – but almost universal – phenomenon. The answer lies with mothers themselves.

You do not need a degree in mothering, nor to spend five years preparing your psyche on top of a mountain. I tried that and failed. The bond is there for you and your child. You as a mother are the supreme expert on your child, so trust your intuitions and never let anyone born of woman, even if he or she needs a double-decker bus to carry their qualifications, say 'You are only a mother.'

A mother's instincts are more than a psychic early warning or unspoken communication system, valuable though those functions are. They are an affirmation above all that even if you don't like your child, you love him. You may have been up for three nights with a squalling bundle, or your toddler may have smeared your only lipstick over the walls. The plaster saint smile slips and you yell terrible things, things the psychologists will tell you have screwed up your child's chances of ever having a satisfactory adult relationship. Ignore them. Such suggestions are psychologists' way of staying in business. Mummy Freud's only mistake was in not clipping little Sigmund round the ear and telling him it was OK to hate her guts – she'd be at the Freud family washtub same time next morning, because someone had to wash all those Freudian slips.

You and your child are linked on a deep level, you are joined soul to soul even if your bodies are clashing like hell. Mothering is very hard work. I would be the last to offer any false job descriptions to would-be applicants for the maternal state. But through this incredible, funny, sometimes tragic, warm, magical mystical and very down to earth mother-child bonding a woman can reach new heights of spiritual awareness as well as the depths of despair. Motherhood has been for me, and for many women, one of the most exciting psychic and spiritual stages of development we have ever experienced.

2

A Mother's Early Warning System

The crucial stage for a mother's instincts is that time before a child can speak for himself. What is so amazing is that a mother in a completely different room from the one her baby is in may detect his silent distress even when others in the same room as the infant notice nothing. This very much knocks on the head the explanation that it is a change in the baby's sounds or even breathing pattern that alerts the mother.

Fortunately, Carolyn Herbert, a mother of five children who lives in Salt Lake City, Utah, did trust her instincts and so saved her child. 'Our first child, born 25 years ago, was bottle-fed and given her own room with all the modern paraphernalia that society deemed necessary. The last four were breast-fed and spent the first four or five years of their life in our room, either in our bed or on a mattress on the floor. I recall many nights when I woke moments before my child needed me.

'I felt an especially close bond with my second daughter, Sarah, and was told by family that we were "too close". I remember one evening when she was about eight months old. I was in the kitchen and she and her sister were in the living room with my husband. I suddenly saw a vision of her choking in my mind, and ran to her. She was choking on a balloon, and though my husband and daughter were there they were not aware of the emergency.'

This is a particularly interesting example, because as I said the mother-baby link was working through walls even though the people right in the room with the baby were totally oblivious to her danger. Furthermore it was a second child, not a first where maternal anxiety would be expected. Carolyn's link with her child persisted, because a similar incident occurred when Sarah was about four. Again Carolyn was the only person alerted to the danger.

'We were in the kitchen preparing dinner. Sarah was standing beside me eating some carrot sticks. In the midst of a normal noisy dinner hour I realized that Sarah was completely quiet, her head was down and she was stamping her foot. It seemed to her older sister Monica, who was twelve at the time, that she was playing. I can't explain what made me feel something was wrong, but just I knew. I stopped what I was doing and turned her round. Her face was purple and she was unable to speak or breathe.

'Monica says she will never forget the look on Sarah's face, and neither shall I. After a moment of sheer panic and total confusion about what to do things suddenly slowed down and I was able to think clearly. I remembered an article I'd read just one week before describing a technique to save the lives of choking victims. It is called the Heimlich Manoeuvre, named after the man that invented it. If a person is choking you stand behind them, wrap your arms around their body and clasp your hands together, then quickly and firmly thrust back up and the foreign object or food pops out. It worked. The carrot sticks just popped right out and her normal colour returned almost immediately. She did start to cry, though, because she felt I had been rough with her and she didn't understand why.

'It was only afterwards I really panicked, thinking of what might have been. Monica is now a mother herself, and while she was staying here with her children I spoke to her of the experience. She remembered it exactly as I do.'

In my view mother and baby are still joined even after the birth, with mother acting as the baby's early warning system because he is unaware of danger. The link seems to be more than telepathy, it combines clairvoyance with premonition, because you can never tell whether the mother has recognized the danger as it is actually happening or has been forewarned in some way so that she arrives on the scene at the last minute. Some people have attempted to analyse this faculty, dividing it into external and internal warnings, such as the mother hearing the baby's psychic cry, or receiving a warning from 'the voice of God' in the words of Annette (the woman who rushed from the cinema to save her infant). In the case of Maria Ferguson of the Isle of Wight, she felt on looking back on a life-threatening experience that it had been her dead grandmother who had issued the warning. But of course at the time she didn't stand round rationalizing. Maria, a presenter with Isle of Wight Radio, responded to a sudden urge that was too swift even for conscious deliberation, and thereby saved her baby from serious injury.

'When my youngest daughter was about nine months old we were following the usual evening ritual most mums know, of sharing a bath filled with ducks and toys. We would splash about together, then I would get out, dry myself and get dressed in the bathroom while Veronica played with the ducks. Then I would get her out and dry and dress her. But on this particular evening I was drying myself with my back to her when suddenly I turned round, snatched her out of the bath and clutched her close to me.

'Veronica screamed with the shock of my grabbing her. Seconds later a huge plant and heavy terracotta pot that was screwed into the ceiling came crashing down. The pot smashed into the water, denting the bath where Veronica had been sitting. I held Veronica until she stopped screaming. I can remember saying, "Thank God, thank God, thank you whoever you are who saved my baby."

'Afterwards I felt it was my dead grandma who had warned me. There are no two ways about it – the baby would have been dead had I not snatched her away at that moment.'

Whichever explanation you choose, these episodes illustrate that a mother should be able to have confidence in her intuition, even if this means sometimes going against professional advice. The mother of Ingrid Millar, a reporter on a top British newspaper, was a trained nurse, but her training proved less effective than Ingrid's instincts in a crisis.

'I was at my mother's house in Scotland,' said Ingrid. 'Rory was four months old. He was propped up in a chair, playing with a brightly coloured box, chewing the corner of it, and I was putting my make-up on. I turned round and noticed his ears were red. Immediately I felt really panicky. I'd never panicked like that before with him, though naturally I worried like most first-time mums. "Phone the doctor," I said to my mother.

'She was a trained nurse, and always erred on the side of caution, but even she thought I was over-reacting. It was nearly Christmas and the central heating was full on. "It's just because the house is so warm and Rory's overheated," she said. "Get the doctor," I insisted. I was really scared. "He won't come out so near to Christmas. Don't worry, Rory's all right. Just take off his jersey and he'll cool down," said my mother. "No, phone an ambulance, now," I insisted. "Well, if you're that worried," my mum said, "Dad will drive you to the doctor."

'The baby was playing quite happily all this time, and didn't seem ill. My mum thought I was being a fussy first-time mother, but I knew something was really wrong. "We've got to phone the ambulance," I remember saying. "We must get him to hospital at once."

'By the time we'd called Dad Rory's ears had swollen to twice their normal size, but he still seemed fine. Mum still thought it wasn't anything serious, but when my dad arrived I told him to take us straight to casualty.

'It was very frosty and about four o'clock in the afternoon. As we went out to the car I could see that Rory's face was starting to swell. By the time we got to the hospital his body had swollen to about twice its normal size and his head was like a football – he looked like a Michelin man. I rushed into casualty shouting: "Help me, please; my baby's very ill," and I realized they were taking me seriously and treating it as an emergency. The doctor injected Rory with an antihistamine drug, but the swelling didn't go down. Rory was kept in hospital overnight, and the doctor said it was the worst allergic reaction he had ever seen. It could have been disastrous because with the swelling his trachea was closing up, so if I hadn't got him to hospital so quickly, well I dread to think what might have happened. I sat by him all night, frightened I'd lose him because he looked so ill. But by morning the swelling had gone down.

'It upsets me even now to think of it, though he is eight. The doctors didn't know what caused the reaction, but they said it might have been that I had taken some antibiotics the week before (I was breast-feeding Rory). I wonder whether he was allergic to the brightly coloured dye on the box he was chewing. Whatever the reason, when his ears went red there was no reason for me to suspect there was anything wrong other than what my mum said, that he was too hot.'

An interesting point in this case is that it was Ingrid who was panicking and not Rory. As she says, throughout the early stages he was playing quite happily and chewing contentedly on everything in sight. Here seems to be another case where the mother had to act as the danger-spotter for a child too young to realize its own peril.

Once the baby starts moving about under its own steam and happily exploring, oblivious to all danger, this sixth sense needs to be even more acute. You can childproof a house until it is as secure as Fort Knox but a baby will still tunnel his way into the most dangerous situation possible, as Maria Campbell of Victoria, Australia, discovered.

'My second son Alexander and I have a special rapport,' she told me. 'One incident has left me with no doubt of the special ties a mother and child have. I was in the kitchen washing dishes and Alex, aged around eleven months (he had started walking by nine-and-a-half months), was running around in our lounge room. Our lounge is very much a childproofed room, so I was confident he could come to no harm. But while I was working I kept getting a fidgety odd feeling that wouldn't go away. It was a very strong feeling of "Do something". I kept trying to ignore it, but then it was like a light that filled a black room. "Alex!" I dropped everything and ran into the other room. There he was, about to put a fistful of sewing needles into his mouth. How my sewing box got into the room I'll never know, as it is always up high in another room. But it was just lucky I got the message that he was in danger.'

Again we have Alex blissfully unaware of his danger and possibly rather annoyed at the time that mum had barged in to stop him seeing what these interesting-looking shiny objects tasted like. We don't know whether this is premonition, telepathy or a guardian angel. But when it is happening you don't stop to work out the metaphysics of it all – leave that to the scientists, philosophers and sceptics – you just move, and fast!

It could be argued that it is sometimes the sudden ominous silence that descends over a house that warns a mother that her child is definitely up to something dangerous. As the old joke runs: "Go and see what Billy is doing – and stop it." I found that quite funny, until I had children.

In the case of Ann Calandro of Harietta, Georgia, a mother of four and a La Leche League leader, the warning came from nowhere, although she could hear her baby burbling happily to her other children. 'When my youngest was eight months old she began to walk around my house. One day I heard her jabbering out the window to my other children, who were playing in the front yard. I had a strong urge to go and get her. I thought to myself that it was a silly urge to have, since she was safe in the house and I could hear her playing. Even so, I could not sit still. I went to her and she was fine. As she turned to look at me, though, she stumbled and the cord to the mini-blinds at the window was around her neck. It tightened at once and she was unable to cry or breathe. I ran and pulled it off and she was fine, although she had a red mark around her neck for a week. I feel there really is something to a mother's intuition; if I had not heeded it she would have suffocated to death.'

Where does the psychic power come from? Some mothers can recall psychic experiences from their own childhood. Maybe we were all psychic as children, as some people believe, but that some of us lose this awareness in the face of disapproving adults. Perhaps motherhood is the time when that dormant potential is re-activated. It is perhaps easier if you can still recall inexplicable experiences from childhood to accept the strange things that motherhood can throw up. Maria Campbell, who prevented her son Alex from swallowing the needles, says that her psychic path started well before motherhood. 'I was ten years old when I told my mum that her father had died. I remember looking at my tea and then having a vision of someone telling mum that her dad had died. It was so strong that I just said, "Mum, Grandpa's dead." Within minutes my aunt was knocking on the door to say my Grandad had died suddenly.

'I now have two children of my own, and feel that this childhood sense has carried into my adult motherhood. When my first born, Veronica, was a baby she would sleep quite soundly, but then I'd wake in the night (or even just be sitting watching television) and I'd get a feeling. I'd say to myself, "No, Veronica, don't wake up." But within maybe thirty seconds of my saying that, she'd wake. I was always annoyed that I could sense when she would wake up. It was almost as if I was waking her just by thinking about her, and not her sending me a message that she was about to wake up.'

The confidence to utilize intuitive feelings rather than going by the book can even be activated by a mother-in-law, although mothers-in-law often get a bad press for interfering and being overly critical. But Norma Ritter's mother-in-law Rose encouraged her to follow her natural instincts and not be bound by books or convention. For Rose had personal experience of the strength of maternal instinct, and had prevented one of her babies from choking by following a seemingly irrational impulse. Norma, a La Leche co-ordinator who lives in Big Flats, New York

State, told me: 'My husband Glenn and I have three children. Dan is fifteen years old, Abigail is thirteen and Chana is nine. I nursed all three children extensively, and feel that I have a strong bond with them.

'With my first child, I thought that it was wrong to bring the baby into bed with me, but my mother-in-law persuaded me at least to have his cot in my room. She had had a dreadful experience with her middle child. The baby was asleep in her cot, in her parents' room. Rose awoke suddenly in the middle of the night, feeling that something was wrong. She ran to the cot and saw that the baby was not breathing. She shook her and started her breathing again, thus avoiding a probable cot death.

'After being told this story you can imagine I took my mother-in-law's advice. I had listened to old wives' tales and was afraid of taking the baby into our bed in case I rolled over on top of him, but I kept his cot at the foot of our bed, and nursed him in a rocking chair when he woke up during the night.

'I feel that our closeness as a family is a result of prolonged nursing and our sleeping so close to one another.'

It is often argued that this instinct is nothing more than a mother hearing, even when asleep, some change in her baby's breathing pattern. But remember the case of Carolyn Herbert, who sensed her baby's distress from the next room. A baby can breathe in a snuffly way, but often his breathing cannot be heard. First-time mothers often check their babies in the night, and even a professional clairvoyant told me that she did not trust her powers with her first child and woke hourly in the night to check her breathing by holding a glass to her lips.

But in the case of Rose it wasn't a first child and she wasn't forever bobbing up and down checking the silences. The criteria of these experiences is that the mother behaves in an uncharacteristic way, often without any apparent prompting. A woman will jump out of sleep or a bath and be there. There is an urgency, an automatic action that is completely different from a mum thinking, 'I can't hear the baby. Maybe I ought to check.'

If you feel this call you will know it, and you will go.

Of course it's not life-and-death situations alone that prompt the cry that is unheard by the physical senses. Sometimes the child just wants you. You are out of earshot – maybe you are relying on other people to tell you if your child needs you. So you ignore the signal from within to go to the infant. Cathy Kyle, of Rotorua in New Zealand, twice failed to trust her intuition when her son Ryan was 13 months old and in hospital having major heart surgery. 'He was in intensive care, and the nurses promised to call me if he woke. I was sleeping elsewhere in the hospital. I woke twice feeling quite upset, and the third time I got up and talked to the night nurse. She suggested I go down to the intensive care unit to see if Ryan was OK. I did and he was awake. In talking to his nurse I discovered that he had been awake twice before, at the very times I had woken and felt upset. That taught me that when I woke I should go down to the unit. He was always awake when I got there.'

You may be lucky enough never to have to face an emergency situation, although many parents do. But whether you are worried about your child's health or have a sudden urge to go to her even if others have assured you they will tell you if the child is distressed, you should go along with your intuition. At the very worst you will look a fool, which is an occupational hazard of being a mother. At best you may save your child's life.

'Why didn't we know we could have saved our child?'

I was faced with this question by a senior reporter on a British national newspaper, who had lost his son in a cot death. Part of this terrible tragedy is that parents can feel unwarranted guilt if they find their infant dead in the morning and then read of others, as with those mentioned in this book, who were able to avert it. I don't know why some parents know in advance and save their child while others don't. They are equally loving, equally good parents, who may regularly wake before the child and are totally in tune with their infant's unvoiced needs. If you hear the call, don't hesitate, but some do not get the chance.

What is the purpose of a mother's instincts in everyday life? Rita Laws of Oklahoma, who had the dubious privilege of psychically sharing her children's toothache, has studied the mother-baby link extensively and sees it as vital to a child's well-being. She told me: 'I believe that this phenomenon has several purposes, not least of which is to afford a helpless baby or younger child extra protection from harm. This might explain why the frequency of events declines as a child gets older. For example, the mother who wakes for no reason only to find her baby has kicked off his blanket is afforded the opportunity to protect him from catching a chill. This has happened to me innumerable times.'

She also advises mothers to note such experiences so that they can show their children the importance of the bond. 'I would advise mothers to record psychic events so that later on they can tell their children about them. I dearly wish my mother had recorded some for me.'

3

Breast-feeding and Instinct

Of course babies aren't those sweet, lovable cooing bundles the media would have us believe, and the psychic channel isn't just reserved for SOS messages. Mums are supposed to be on duty twenty-four hours a day, and if baby is hungry, fed up or simply decides that only mum will do, the yells will come through loud and clear – and not just with the force of his lungs. You may be out of earshot but you are not out of 'mindshot'. Babies can put you on a very long invisible lead, especially when it comes to feeding time. It may not be a matter of life and death to you, but to the little chap with an empty belly it certainly is, and babies are rather fussy about what they eat and who feeds them. If baby decides that 'breast is best' then you cannot fob him off with a bottle of expressed milk, and his psychic cries of protest can drown out even the most ear-splitting rock concert.

Mum might be having a bit of time off, but this is definitely not in the contract as the baby sees it, and so she may find herself on the receiving end of a telepathic tantrum. Rita Laws says: 'I was at a Hall and Oates concert in 1985. It was the first time I had ever left my third birthchild, Joaquin, who had been born the previous September. I was uneasy leaving him, but my aunt lived very near to the concert venue. I expressed some milk for a bottle, and when we left he was very happy. I had every reason to believe he was fine. I spent the whole concert wanting to phone my aunt but I forced myself not to. I was trying to be "practical".

'For two hours I sat on the edge of my seat unable to relax at all but with no idea why. All my senses were on edge but my hearing seemed particularly acute. In fact the music seemed so loud it was painful. Placing tissue in my ears finally allowed me a little comfort. Then suddenly every muscle in my body relaxed simultaneously. I fell back in my chair feeling sleepy, removed the tissue from my ears and at last began to enjoy the music. The last part of the concert was great.

'When I went to pick up my son he was sleeping peacefully, but my aunt and uncle looked haggard. The baby had screamed for two hours, so loudly it had hurt their ears. He had refused the bottle of breast-milk and all of his favourite toys. Then, exhausted, he had fallen into a deep sleep. Mother and son had been linked all along.'

Babies may seem to be simple little bundles of unconnected reflexes, but they do care about more than just food. Back in the 1950s Harry F. Harlow and his colleagues at the University of Wisconsin demonstrated scientifically what all mothers know automatically: that babies need mothers for cuddling and comforting as much as for food. Harlow put baby monkeys in a cage with two dummy mothers. One was cloth and cuddly, the other was made of wire but had a 'nipple' offering milk. Although the babies went to the wire monkey to feed, they would immediately run back to the cloth monkey for comfort.

Maria Campbell of Australia did not leave a cloth monkey for her baby but rather a loving grandmother, plus a bottle of breast-milk and a dummy. But this was not enough to placate the little fellow.

'When Alex was only a few weeks old my husband and I decided to go to the pictures one night. I was breast-feeding, so I expressed milk into a bottle for my mother-in-law to give Alex should he need it. He always took a dummy, so I thought he would accept the bottle. The whole time I was out, about three hours, I felt agitated, restless and totally fidgety. I just wanted to get back to Alex. I didn't know why.

'On our return Alex was beetroot. He had screamed continually. My mother-in-law said he didn't want the bottle, had refused his dummy, and just wouldn't settle. As soon as I picked him up he nuzzled into me and wanted a feed. While I fed him and as he gave delightful little burps of contentment afterwards it occurred to me that I had literally dumped him and run. So the next time I had to leave him, even though he was only six weeks old I would "tell" him what I was doing and where I was going. I'd spend a few minutes holding him and giving him comforting thoughts along the lines of "Grandma will hold you warm and cozy and loving. Mummy will be back soon. Not long. Mummy loves you." It worked every time. My mother-in-law couldn't believe it: the monster had turned into an angel.

'Alex and I have such a special relationship, it's just beautiful. He only says about three words (he's sixteen months old) but just knowing I can communicate with him silently is wonderful.'

Rita Laws says incidents such as these are not uncommon among mothers, and among fathers, too, though she has found parents reluctant to discuss such incidents. 'We as a society should celebrate – not hide – the psychic link that exists between parents and their children. These invisible bonds are just one more indication of how special the love is between mothers, fathers and their sons and daughters.'

One common factor of the women who tell these stories is that they have breast-fed. What is the magic that flows with mother's milk?

In a tribe of American Indians, the Zinacantecos in southeastern Mexico, the sociologist T. Berry Brazelton[1] discovered that it was common for mothers to lactate *before* their babies cried. These women never had to face the scenario all too familiar to most of us: baby screaming, mum getting upset, baby won't feed, mum gets more uptight.

But this pre-yell lactation is not an ability restricted to American Indians. Furthermore, this kind of 'fine-tuning' may

[1] T. Berry Brazelton, 'Implications of Infant Development among Mayan Indians of Mexico', in P.H. Leiderman et al., *Culture and Infancy – Variations in the Human Experience*, Academic Press, 1977.

actually develop as the mother's confidence in her own instincts increases. In Newcastle, Rachel Hey found a similar effect with her son Jacob, who was born on January 2, 1991. 'He has very irregular night feeds, but I find I always wake, leaking milk, just before he begins to stir. This has only happened for the last three weeks. I used to only wake when he was crying. Now he never even whimpers before he is fed.

'At first I leaked milk from both breasts. Now I find I only leak milk from the breast that is due to be fed from (I only feed from one breast at a time).'

As for Rita Laws, who is of English, Irish, German and Cherokee and Choctaw Indian descent, she found that even as a working mother her milk kept flowing and the psyche calling. Rita breast-fed her three birthchildren and some of her seven adopted children, so for her the breast-link is of immense importance. Rita has recorded numerous occasions when she responded to the unheard distress signal of one of her infants, even when she was far away. 'My second birthchild, Tim, was born in 1982, and was totally breast-fed until he was seven months old and was not weaned for several years. I returned to my teaching job when he was eight weeks old, expressing milk at work to give the babysitter. Tim would cry at irregular intervals during the working day, but these intervals always coincided with my let-down reflexes at work a block away. I was a La Leche League Leader for four years, and I sat in on many meetings when this "breast-link" was discussed – and I heard many women tell stories similar to mine. It is common for many women to admit to having many more psychic experiences than usual while they are pregnant or nursing. I have heard midwives say that the woman in labour is the most psychic of all people. As her body opens to birth, her sixth sense opens up too.

'I remember once I was writing multiplication problems on the blackboard at school when I felt the familiar let-down tingle in my breasts. Moments later the milk had soaked through. Quickly I gathered up my jumper which I kept on the back of my chair for just such occurrences.

'It was only 10 a.m., and only minutes before I had expressed several ounces of milk for my three-month-old son, so I was puzzled. I hadn't been thinking about him, hadn't heard him cry, so why the let-down reflex? At noon I raced the two blocks to the sitter, anxious to nurse and cuddle my infant.

'As I settled down to feeding him the sitter, an elderly woman who thought I was silly to go on nursing, began to complain, "Your baby cries too much. He wants to be held all the time. Just this morning at 10 he had a crying fit the likes of which I've never heard before." Now I understood. The baby had needed me and I had responded.'

Just to be sure, Rita decided on a little experiment. 'For the next few days, the sitter and I recorded the times of the unexpected let-downs and the inconsolable crying fits. The crying always preceded the gush of milk by five minutes or so.

'I always knew when my babies were about to wake from a nap five minutes before it happened, even though the babies napped at different times every day and for varying lengths of times. My doubting husband became convinced after several correct predictions in a row. Once the infants grew older, say about seven months of age, I found I was no longer able to make any predictions about their waking times, but until then I was unerringly correct.'

Working mothers in other societies share this problem; they respond to their baby's cry for food even though they may be miles away and can't possibly feed their infant. In their book *Only Mothers Know* (Greenwood Press, 1985), Dana Raphael and Flora Davis write of Odani, who lives in Sagada, an Igorot village in the mountain region of northern Luzon in the Philippines. Talking about the birth of her first child she described how, in common with most other Igorot women who farmed, she had to go back to the fields when her son was two months old, leaving the child with his grandmother. She described how sometimes when she was in the fields her breasts would tingle as the ejection reflex occurred. Igorot mothers, she said, believe that this is a sign that miles away in the village the baby is hungry and crying, so if they possibly can, they hurry home.

Of course the scientists (usually male) would have us believe that it's all to do with biological rhythms. They obviously have captured in the laboratory that rarest of all creatures: the baby who wakes every four hours on the dot, perfectly synchronized with mum's hormonal tap. But as Rita found, the flow had nothing to do with regular feeding times. Vicky, a maths lecturer in Southampton, would put her baby to nap in the pram at the bottom of her long garden during the day. Suddenly Vicky would find that her jumper was wet, and she would know the baby was crying even though the infant had no regular feeding times during the day. Several times when Vicky's own mother was there, Vicky would be in another room, completely out of sight or ear-shot of the garden. But Vicky would need only to notice that her jumper was wet to say: 'The baby is awake', though the baby might have been fed only an hour before. Her mother would not believe Vicky, and would creep down the garden to prove the baby was still asleep. But to her annoyance, as soon as she was within sight of the pram she would see the baby's mouth opening and closing in rage.

Maria Cadaxa, a midwife in Tucson, Arizona, commented: 'Regarding nursing, the let-down connection between mother and baby seems to be universal. I have yet to encounter a mother who has not experienced it at least once. The most common phenomenon is the milk coming in just seconds before the baby's first squeal of hunger, often after a long nap. The timing is so coincidentally precise it can't be put down to any "natural" interval between feedings, as the occurrences span a wide range of time between one hour and two and a half, the milk coming in precisely before the child wakes up.

'Another curious reflex is letting down milk when any child cries, even if one's own child is not present. If one's own is present, however, this does not seem to happen.'

Although breast-feeding seems to strengthen maternal instinct, it is not the only thing that does. Dana Raphael, Director of the Human Lactation Center in Westport, Connecticut, who has spent more than 35 years observing thousands of mothers and babies, warns against trying to simplify the issues of bonding to a breast- vs. bottle-feeding dichotomy.

'We are not chickens, nor goats, where, I admit, patterns of relationships seem to depend somewhat on early mother/infant behaviour. We are human beings, and appear to be able to fall in love – or to bond – even at the age of 90. I know of mothers who breast-fed (promoted these days as a good way of connecting with one's baby) yet hated their kids, and others who bottle-fed and had loving relationships, and still others who breast-fed and hated it but did it and still love the creature that made those early days so unpleasant.

'I know fathers, who of course do not breast-feed, who were unable to see their children for the first several months yet adore them. And ditto for all the mothers and fathers and children in the less developed countries, except they have a harder time because so often mothers must choose which child is to get the little bit of extra food and live and which they must break their hearts over and bury.

'All parents love their children, so how dare we say that village women who breast-feed are any better (at bonding) than the inner-city mother who struggles as well.'

Indeed, one of the most striking cases I came across was of a mother who was unable to breast-feed her infant because she was in a coma. Newspapers in June 1991 carried the story of Caroline Head from Bradford, an 18-year-old mother who had been in a coma for two months after falling 25 feet down steps at a club in the city. Doctors had warned that she might never regain consciousness because of the severity of her head injuries. But her mother, Mrs Christine Wilson, regularly took Caroline's 13-week-old daughter Danielle to see Caroline, and kept putting the child in Caroline's arms although she was unconscious.

'I also played tape recordings of Danielle crying and gurgling all the time I was with her,' Mrs Wilson told reporters. 'I was hoping Danielle might reach Caroline in a way the doctors couldn't.'

Then Caroline suddenly opened her eyes and asked: 'Can I hold my baby?'

'It is a miracle that it has worked,' said Mrs Wilson, 'and just goes to show the bond between a mother and her baby.'

It can perhaps be argued by sceptics that there was nothing 'magical' about this recovery. Doctors say that the presence of family or friends in the same room as a patient in a coma can sometimes bring about a recovery, because the sounds, smell or feel of them somehow penetrate the fog surrounding the victim's brain. But the fact of the matter is that the child roused her mother in a way that medical science could not. The link is important for what it does, not how well it satisfies abstract criteria, for it never operates in an abstract situation but in those where love is the key.

Another issue often related to the breast-feeding question about which mothers and scientists fall out is night-time waking. What is it that makes a mother wake seconds before her child to avoid the yelling and panic that can disrupt the quiet harmony? Again, mothers and babies can be very inconvenient and refuse to fit in with theory, even the very best theories such as those of Dr William Sears, author of *Nighttime Parenting* (Penguin, 1985), who has collected lots of evidence about the synchronization of mums' and babies' sleep patterns. This shared rhythm, he believes, leads mum to wake just before the baby does. This may well account for many cases of night-time waking, and is of course enhanced by all those hormones activated by breast-feeding and tactile contact. So if mum breast-feeds and sleeps with the little one (a situation I would recommend if the mother has back-up to care for her while she cares for the baby) the two clocks tick in harmony. But of course there are the many other rogue cases of mums who sleep in different rooms, whose babies have no regular waking or feeding patterns, and yet who still consistently wake just before their infants do. I even found dads who woke seconds before the baby while mum slumbered on. As Dr Sears commented to Carl Jones, author of *From Parent to Child, the Psychic Link* (Warner Books, 1989): 'I feel there must be something going on that has so far eluded all the medical studies.' And that is a fair comment on the mother-baby link in general.

The simple answer to the question of maternal night-waking, that a mother unconsciously heard a whimper in her sleep, would in some cases require a sense of hearing that came close to that of a bat, or alternatively stone deafness. For what of women who sleep through a toddler's yells but wake regularly before the baby even murmurs?

Helena Boutal, a British La Leche Leader, recalls that when her daughter Amy was still a baby she put her in a different room at the end of the corridor to see if she would sleep better. Helena slept through when her toddler Suzy woke in the night, though Suzy's room was nearer to hers than Amy's. In fact it was her husband Chris who woke up and went to Suzy, and the exhausted Helena was not disturbed at all. But if Amy so much as stirred, Helena would sit bolt upright. Yet Chris did not hear the baby at all. This happened before Amy was six months old.

Tamara Raetz comes from Mountain View, California. She is a member of the Mid-Peninsula Mothers of Twins Clubs, and has identical girls, Emily and Elizabeth. 'Until my daughters were about 15 months old,' she said, 'I was always able to tell when one or both were waking, through two closed doors and without the benefit of a nursery monitor. I would feel a sort of stirring in my head – this is hard to explain – followed almost directly by the sound of their crying.

'Also I began to sense a connection between my thoughts and their waking, as if thinking about them woke them up. I would often startle visitors by starting for the door seconds before their crying began. Even my husband was surprised.

'Now my daughters, aged two, sleep deeply, and I no longer

prevent myself thinking about them while they sleep, although I can still tell in the early mornings whether or not they are awake, though all is quiet. I have been thoroughly "explained to" by friends who find all sorts of explanations, but I thought perhaps you might find the experiences not only believable but useful as well.'

The problem with explanations – from both friends and professional experts – are that they may hold true only for a segment of experience where factors may be constant. But they are applied blanket-like to all women's night-time waking and feeding experiences, ignoring those factors which do not fit the pattern. Once a woman becomes a mother, the physiological and psychological become confused and compounded with the entangling of the mysterious mother/baby communion. All the analysts are left with is a pile of very neat statistics, which any self-respecting baby whose mother's instincts had been called into question would chew or do worse with before crawling off to share with his mum the wonders of a universe so infinite it can only be marvelled at.

Instead of maternal waking wouldn't it be wonderful to will the baby back to sleep instead of having to feed him? Magic? Well, yes, according to Cathy Kyle of Rotorua in New Zealand, who found that when she was desperate for a good night's sleep she could will him back to sleep when he stirred. Cathy, as we saw in the last chapter, had at first ignored but then learned to trust her instincts, and used them to her advantage. 'I used to think it was just good luck. It started when I was very tired. I would lie in bed and think about how tired I was. Then I would get up to see to him. But one night I was so tired I just lay there and pleaded with him (in my mind) to go to sleep. To my amazement I noticed his cry became less persistent than usual, and so I started to "tell" him (all still in my thoughts) what a good boy he was and that it was night-time and time to sleep. He stopped crying and went back to sleep. He is 23 months old now, and I can still do this.'

It would be greatly appreciated if Cathy would bottle this and send it to us less tuned-in mums.

The intuitive link is of course a two-way street even in the early days, and it's hard to distinguish which psyche is doing the waking. And, as we have seen, it's not only the night-time waking that is the problem. Mum relies on baby's nap times, however irregular, to fit in all those little luxuries like eating, napping herself, and indulging in those half-forgotten activities with her partner that started the whole business.

What of the experiences of Joan Cannon of New South Wales in Australia? 'The first thing I noticed was that Jode always woke the moment I went to put any food in my mouth – not just occasionally, I mean every time. If I changed my eating times, he'd change his waking times. This went on for the first three months.

'Then at night we'd all be in bed and he'd be very quiet and I'd be worrying whether everything was OK. So I'd lie there and think really hard, "Jode, make a noise" and without fail he'd groan or move or even sigh, and then I could sleep. I seem to have a knack of checking on him just as he's waking. I don't know why I check but he's always starting to wake.

'His latest trick is waking the minute my husband and I contemplate sneaking some time for ourselves to have sex. It doesn't matter how tired he is or what time it is, he just wakes and refuses to go back to sleep. I think this might happen because I'm subconsciously thinking "I hope he doesn't wake up" and he's receiving strong messages from me. He never wakes if we're watching telly or talking, only when we're heading for the bedroom. I strongly believe Jode and I are on the same wavelength. We know each other so well.'

Maybe Jode has been practising psychic birth control!

Joan wrote to me again, telling me that she was not waking with Jode regularly these days but only when he was ill. On these occasions she still wakes up before he does. 'I'm sure that because he's older now he doesn't need to communicate at night except when he's ill,' she said. This leaves rather a gap in the theory that the sleep patterns of mother and baby are synchronized causing the mother to wake before her child. It is again the unvoiced need of the child that seems to communicate itself to the waiting mother.

James E. Peron, Director of the Childbirth Education Foundation in Richboro, Pennsylvania, says: 'We do indeed agree with you that there exists a very special psychic bond between a mother and her young child. There are, of course, those who dismiss any such link. There are even those who argue that it is not necessary for infants to "bond" with their parents at birth. Yet if we look at the relationship of mother and offspring in the animal world, we see that this innate communication link is highly developed. Are we to believe then that it does not exist in the highest form of mammalian life?'

Of course there has been much research into the top half of the problem, but what about the bottom half, the psychic question? Is there such a thing as psychic potty training? Ugandan women, who carry their infants in slings next to their breasts or on their backs for hours on end, neither swaddle them nor use nappies. Yet to the amazement of foreigners, the babies never soil or wet themselves or their mothers. One doctor's wife inquired how the mothers knew when the babies needed to go to the bushes to relieve themselves. 'How do *you* know when *you* want to go?' the Ugandan women asked her.

Of course, they weren't letting on that they practise until they can tell when the baby is about to urinate or defecate. Then they swing the baby out of their packs at the precise moment, hold the child over the dirt and wait for the baby to finish. New mothers, who don't have this ability honed, are routinely and good-naturedly teased by the other mothers when they get their backs soiled. Our old friend synchronicity again? Or magic? As a mother who has spent a fortune on nappies and been caught out so many times, I wish I could learn this technique.

In an ideal world every mother would have the necessary support, time and emotional and physical security to find breast-feeding fulfilling. There is no doubt that breast-feeding is a wonderfully bonding experience, and because it is so automatic and instant – an extension of the womb's field-kitchen system – it does allow mum and baby to get on with the business of communicating on an intuitive level without physical hassles getting in the way. For when a baby stirs, mum, whether psychically or hormonally, is alerted from sleep at night or diverted from other (less vital, in baby's opinion) activities during the day, and so is ready and waiting. Instant satisfaction and no anxiety with mum dashing round heating bottles to the tune of baby's bawling. Hormones aside, breast-feeding enables everyone to get on with things of the spirit. So any psychic communication must be easier if you breast-feed. Having tried breast- and bottle-feeding I found that, in addition to the nutritional advantages and the resulting reduction in infant infections, breast-feeding was more pleasurable for me as well as easier. It gave a special intimacy to the mother-baby link that was magic in itself. Having said that, my most frequent psychic bond experiences occurred with a child I wasn't able to breast-feed.

So if breast is the best but not the only psychic channel, where does that leave us? If you breast-feed and sleep with your baby the maternal hormones will flow and open the channel for other less tangible streams of communication to flow. But if you're tired and alone, living in overcrowded conditions, and you can't get away from a yelling baby for even an hour in the day, then these theories can make you feel a bit of a failure, and that's not fair. I know because I tried to breast-feed my second child while my world was collapsing around my ears. What's left then if the milk dries up and your body screams for a bit of peace?: Mother-magic, which takes over where all the theories fall short and stops you throttling the child, which keeps you high when you are hallucinating from lack of sleep. I can't explain it or prove it but I've felt it, as have the hundreds of women who've talked or written to me. Let's just be thankful that it exists.

4

Toddlers and Telepathy

The mother-baby link does not dry up with your milk. But the incidents that prove its existence can be so fleeting that unless you note them at the time you can miss them. So often a mother will just feel panic or a sense of urgency that causes her to drop her basket in the middle of the supermarket and head for home as fast as possible.

In February 1991 I had gone to Newport, the Isle of Wight's county town and about ten miles from my home. My husband John was collecting the older children from school just before three o'clock, taking three-year-old Bill with him. As John is away for much of the week, I was glad just to go off without the children and wander round the town, and I intended to do the week's shopping at the supermarket. About half-past four I reached the supermarket. I was moving slowly, enjoying the bliss of not having Bill riding gladiator-style on the trolley, hurling goods about and yelling his head off (he is suffering what a health professional called 'management problems', which means he is just a particularly diabolical toddler – he enjoyed the terrible twos so much he merged them into the threatening threes). I suddenly started to feel uncomfortable. I kept thinking: 'I'm frightened,' which made no sense because here I was walkabout with the glories of the frozen-food cabinets stretched temptingly before me. Then I was stricken by the most terrible pains – something akin to labour – which got progressively worse over the next few minutes. Unable to endure them any longer I abandoned the idea of shopping and headed for the nearest check-out point with what I'd got so far, pausing irrationally to buy a toy car for Bill. I never buy a toy for only one child (it

41

would provoke a riot), but my thoughts were only of Bill. After what seemed an age, and during which I clung to my trolley and wondered whether to ask for help or just leave everything, I reached the counter. The assistant was talking about a special offer in the local newspaper which would reduce my shopping bill, but I was unable to concentrate. Once outside I felt uncertain about what to do next. Should I phone home, have a rest in the nearest cafe until the pain passed, or return home immediately? Getting to the car, loading it and driving out seemed to happen in slow motion. I narrowly avoided a collision with another car, and continued to feel panicky until I had been driving along for five minutes, when suddenly I relaxed and the pains disappeared, as if by magic. I had left the supermarket at about 5.10 p.m. by the clock outside; the whole experience had lasted about half an hour.

When I got home I noticed Bill was dressed in a warm sleeping suit – unusual for that time of night – and John, trying to seem casual, asked me if I had had any 'premonitions' while I was out. I told him what had happened, and then he told me what had occurred while I had been away.

Just after 4.30 p.m. he had been walking the kids home from school alongside the River Yar, which flows through woods near our home. It was an unusually warm day, so he had stopped by the river to let the children play among the trees, and made the fatal mistake (for a parent) of letting his guard down for a second. Suddenly Bill made a lunge towards the river, which was not very wide but quite deep with the winter rains. Bill probably meant to stop at the last minute, but didn't. John hurled himself into the water and dragged out a howling Bill, put him in his pushchair and hurried all the kids home.

Being a journalist he automatically made a quick note of the time, 4.45, which was approximately when my panic attack started. By around 5.10 Bill had been bathed and soothed and had stopped yelling.

Supermarkets seem remarkably common places for tuning into

the vibes of a young child in trouble. Maybe scientists can forge a link between all that electricity humming and psychic channels. Marian McCahe from County Dublin told me: 'In July 1984, my young daughter Margaret participated in a local Summer Project in Dublin. I dropped her at the school so she could go off with a group of other children on a train ramble to Howth. There were two university students in charge of the group.

'Nearly 30 minutes later, while waiting in the frozen food department of my local supermarket, I was suddenly seized with a feeling of extreme apprehension, fear and dread. I felt as though a black cloud had descended upon me, and my heart sank. I had never felt such awful despair before or since. The feeling passed in about ten minutes, and I passed it off possibly as low blood sugar and forgot about it. A few hours later I returned to the school to collect Margaret. I discovered that due to a sudden strike on the railway the ramble had been cancelled, but that as one of the students had a friend who worked in a fish-processing plant he had rung him and the friend had sent a tiny fishing boat to bring the children down the Liffey river and out to the plant. The time I felt that awful fear and dread corresponded to the time Margaret was making her way down an oily, seaweed-covered slip to the little boat. She told me she was terrified but that the student could not let her stay behind as there was no one to care for her. Thank God there were no mishaps.'

When a mother's instincts are running on full power they cannot be fooled. To try to spare a mother's feelings someone might tell her that junior is safe when she makes a frantic phone call home, but she will know better than that, as the story of Elaine C. Emmi of Salt Lake City, Utah, shows.

In 1983 Elaine and her husband were living in the Los Angeles area with their son Matt, who was almost five. 'I was in Palm Springs setting up a conference for the Nature Conservancy for their annual meeting. I had taken my neighbour along for the ten days away from home. Matt would spend the mornings at his pre-school and the afternoons with a friend from school.

Then his dad would pick him up on the way home from work. As my neighbor and I were getting ready to drive back to LA from Palm Springs we decided to get a quick bite to eat so that we would miss the rush-hour traffic. As we were waiting for our order in the restaurant I had the most horrible feeling come over me. I told my neighbor I must call home to check on Matt. She kept telling me not to worry, but I knew things were not right. I put in a call home, and when no one answered and the answer-phone didn't come on I was even more certain things were not well. So I proceeded to call my neighbor's husband. He told me he didn't know anything (later he told me he had lied about this but that at the time he hadn't wanted to upset me before I spent two-and-a-half hours on the road).

'We ate our dinner in silence and left soon after. The drive home was the worst in my life, as I was still convinced something terribly wrong had happened.

'My neighbour's husband came out to meet us as we drove up. He then told me that Matt had fallen through a glass door and was going into surgery shortly. He had severed many of the tendons in his right hand. I got to the hospital shortly before his surgery, and so I was able to be with Matt for a couple of minutes. All turned out well, and now at age twelve he has full use of his hand.'

An instance of this psychic lie-detector at work between a mother and her grown-up daughter was given by Claire Roberts of Miranda, New South Wales. She said: 'I left home in Victoria when I was 18 (I'm 36 now), but my mother and I still have a strong bond even though I live hundreds of miles away. I can't tell you how many times over the last 18 years she has rung up in moments when I'm experiencing a crisis to ask me if everything is all right. On the morning that my ex-husband and I decided to break up she rang up, and wouldn't believe me when I said everything was fine.'

Joe Cooper, the social science lecturer and parapsychologist who has written *The Mystery of Telepathy* (Constable, 1982), sees no problems with this kind of maternal 'crisis' telepathy as it is sometimes called. He says, 'Telepathy uses the language of the soul. With mother and child there is tremendous soul-flow, as there is between people who are in love.

'To give a simple example, an Open University student of mine when aged seven stepped out from behind a bus and was knocked unconscious by a car. She found herself above her body – as though her soul had been extracted leaving her body ticking over – and travelled in an instant to her mother who was peeling potatoes in the kitchen a few houses away. She conveyed her plight to her mother, who put down the peeler and went out of the house and round the corner to the scene of the accident. The girl came round and found her mother looking down at her.'

But the telepathy does not only warn of danger. In a time of apparent crisis it can also work to reassure a mother that things are not as bad as they seem. Louise, mother of Craig, two, and Alex, four, and who lives in the south of England, told me: 'It seems silly sometimes but you should listen to yourself, trust your instincts and develop them. I know last summer Alex got lost on the housing estate where I live. I was starting to cry and get upset when I thought: "Wait a minute, this is all superficial. I know he's all right because I can feel he's still there. He hasn't gone from me." So I relaxed, and sure enough before long he turned up at a friend's house. I knew he wasn't in danger; my instinct told me. We can't see electricity but we have to pay the bills so we know it exists. A mother's instinct and telepathy are the same.'

She described the link this way: 'as if the cord between you was cut physically but not psychologically'.

Once a child has language then the bond becomes more of a two-way process and moves closer to the conventional definition of telepathy. However, it remains a telepathy that does not conform to laboratory card-guessing experiments between a bored child and a researcher who often regards the subject as a rather unsavoury member of the lower orders of the animal kingdom.

It can happen that the child uses this link to reassure her mother. Donata Glassmeyer lives in Mainville, Ohio. Her daughter, now six, was born when Donata was 38. She believes that 'the intense birthing and bonding Hope and I experienced contributed to her abilities to communicate with me and her father on deep, unconventional levels.

'As early as a year old Hope could point to an object, particularly the bathtub drain handle, minutes before it would break. Today she can often tell who is calling before I answer the phone, or whether her father is home long before we pull into the driveway.

'When she was almost two I went out for the afternoon, leaving her at home with her sister. While on the highway I was forced off the road by a truck. Although I was not injured the incident was upsetting because the driver did not stop.

'When I arrived home Hope and I went out into the backyard to play in the sandbox. I sat in a lawn chair vividly recalling the truck incident in my mind as I wrote a letter of complaint to the company whose truck had caused the near-accident. After a few minutes my little girl, who could barely talk, said, "No big truck come in this yard, Momma." I had not mentioned a word to her or her sister about the event, but Hope had been able to pick up the information simply by being close to me. For days she assured me that our house and yard were safe from big trucks.'

We do not know at what point a child begins to home in on his mother's distress, but as we have said it is only when the child can put thoughts into words that we become aware of this ability. Mary, now a mother herself and living in County Cork, can still recall this link between herself and her mother. 'When I was young, my mother had taken my brother to our summer place to do some work on the house. About five o'clock in the afternoon I knew something dreadful had happened to my mother. The feeling was so strong I knelt down and started to pray. My mother sometimes had a tendency to choke, so my immediate thought was it was that. But later I heard that she and my brother had gone for a walk to the beach and that at about five o'clock she had fallen down the concrete steps leading onto the beach and had hurt herself badly though not dreadfully.

'I never had the feeling again until my own son was about three. We had moved house, and although we always meant to fit locks to the upstairs windows we never got round to it. My mother and sister had come over and we were sitting having afternoon tea and talking when I suddenly stopped in mid-sentence. "I've got to go to the little one," I said and rushed upstairs to my husband's office, to find my son at the open window. He had climbed onto my husband's desk, somehow opened the window, and was within two inches of falling out from the upper floor.'

Jung recognized that the mother-baby link was beyond psychology. He believed that for a long time after the birth mother and child form a psycho-physical (and later a psychic) unity, and normally, he said, a strong psychic bond persists throughout the child's early years. It has its roots as much in the unconscious as in consciousness.

If a mother can harness this force for her own ends it can be very fruitful, as Lilian Skeels found when she was a little girl in war-time England. The magic pictures from her mother's mind lit up the blackout for her.

'I grew up in Cheshire during the war,' Lilian said, 'and though I was only little we used to have to walk miles from the town to our house through the blackout. I was a heavy lump, so mum sussed a way to make me walk. She would put me into a sort of hypnotic trance with her voice and tell me films, not just the stories but the pictures as well, she would put them in my mind. It was so lovely I didn't want to wake up, and then suddenly we'd be home and my little legs aching. The trouble was that after the war, when I went to see these films for myself they seemed old hat. They were scene for scene what mum had shown me.'

More often than not as the child grows older it is she who surprises mother with a sudden flash of telepathy which is not triggered by a crisis but springs up in an everyday situation. This would seem to occur because children do not always appear to realize that their thoughts and their parents' thoughts should be separate entities: they seem to 'mind-hop' – jumping in and out of your thoughts at unguarded moments. It seems to be a completely random process over which neither they nor you have any control. And this ability appears to fade as education teaches them that they should not be able to have it.

Ann Burbidge of Leicester recalls: 'Years ago my eldest child, then aged four, was playing in our lounge, cutting pictures out of an old catalogue. I went into the kitchen to cook, and was idly thinking how much I would like a ring with stones set all round the band. A few minutes later my daughter came into the room and said she had a present for me. Out of all the things she could have cut out of the catalogue she had brought me a ring almost identical to the one I had been mentally designing.'

This 'mind-hopping' can be a bit of a giveaway when you are trying to keep a secret, as Bernice, living in Scotland and now a grandmother, found with her son Paul. 'Paul was something over three years old, and we were having our dinner. He was feeding himself and daddy didn't come home for midday dinner so conversation was at a minimum. The dining table was directly in front of the window. The year was waning and colder weather settling in and it occurred to me it would be a good idea to move the table away from possible draughts – but where? The obvious wall was taken up by a tall chest which would block all the light if we did a straight swap.

'My husband hated change and upheaval, so it would be a non-starter if I consulted him. I should have to present him with a *fait accompli*. So as I ate I planned a total rearrangement of the furniture without speaking a word. Later that afternoon a friend called in for tea and a chat. As we sat by the fire Paul suddenly said, "Mummy's going to move the furniture. She's going to put the table over there . . .", and went on to describe quite accurately all the changes I had planned.'

For Julia of Berkshire it is not a case of one particular incident that stands out but a process which has grown since conception and continues all the time. Laurence is her second child. 'I knew the moment I had conceived him. I wrote to tell my friend I was pregnant the next morning. It was strange because I had two years of fertility treatment before I conceived my first child, Laura, and I was booked to go and see the doctor for more treatment. I said to the doctor on the first visit, "I think you should be careful examining me, just in case." To his surprise I was pregnant. Throughout the pregnancy Laurence was my son. I never thought for one moment he was a girl. Laura was much-loved but Laurence was a part of me. I knew exactly what he would be like, and I was right, down to the last detail. I always saw him at about three years old, and when he was three he was the child I had imagined.

'Once he was born I woke before he did and was totally in tune with his needs and emotions. I know a second child is easier anyway, but this was almost magical. As he grew, Laurence read my every thought. I would think, "I wonder where I put my sewing box?", and he would be there from another room with it in his little hands. Or I would notice a mark on the furniture and think "I must polish that," and there instantly was Laurence from another part of the house with my polish. No words were necessary, nor even visual contact.'

One thing I noticed about 'routine' telepathy, as opposed to 'crisis' telepathy, was that the parents most prone to these everyday excursions into their grey cells were those who didn't dash about frantically stimulating the kids with lots of toys and activities but rather were content to let the children get on with childhood in their own way. I suppose this gave the kids the space to let it happen.

Tom Anderson from Summerland, British Columbia, who has studied both North American and Mexican birth and child-rearing practices, wholeheartedly endorses the relaxed approach, which he says should start right from the time of birth. 'It's amazing what one can learn simply by not meddling in natural functions. The birth of my daughter Kitty was so quick, easy and wonderful, and Kitty herself was such an amazing creature, everything I thought I knew about birth and about babies had to be discarded. I've since had many opportunities to confirm that what I observed and experienced was in no way abnormal; quite the contrary. My daughter Holly's birth and childhood, though much different from Kitty's, further enhanced my understanding of what is normal and what isn't.

'Medical professionals and most parents just look at me strangely if I mention that my children didn't cry at birth, that they had only breast-milk for the first six months, that they never tasted "baby food", that they never fussed, threw tantrums or otherwise misbehaved, that there was never a time to eat or go to bed and that we never owned a cot, a buggy, walker or pushchair.

'I remember clearly how both Kitty and Holly responded to my thoughts even when they were still tiny babies, and I remember especially when my partner told me of something astonishing that occurred one evening.

'Holly must have been between one and two; she had her own little sleeping space then, near to her mum but separated by a partition. She had gone to bed and was singing to herself, as she often did, while her mum picked up a book to read. The book was about Switzerland. Holly stopped singing, then quietly but very clearly said, "Switzerland". For several minutes Holly continued to pronounce words that her mother came across as she read on. Then Holly apparently fell asleep and that was the end of it.

'I've always wondered how common this might be, perhaps only occurring where bonding has not been compromised or perhaps occurring but going unnoticed where bonding is poor. Scientifically dismissible, I expect, until such time as "hard evidence" is produced.'

Chris McDermott from High Wycombe in Buckinghamshire

is another very relaxed, open person. She told me when I met her: 'When my son Michael was young (he is now 21) we had a strong rapport, and he would pick up my desires and wishes without my saying anything. Once when he was three we were walking through the woods chatting about the leaves and the squirrels and I was thinking, "I wish we could go to Slough to visit my friends the Benedictine nuns." We only went twice a year but I loved to go, and suddenly felt the desire to see them again. Michael had been only two the last time we had gone to visit so I doubt whether he would have had any memory of it. But I was thinking about them and wishing quite strongly I could go and see them. I can still recall it, walking between the beech trees when Michael suddenly said, "Wouldn't it be lovely to go this Saturday to see the nuns?" He was an articulate child, but I don't know what made him say that for I know there had been no mention of them. The ability to pick up my wishes seemed to fade as he got older and went to school.

'I was perhaps closest to Michael, my third son. He had to go to nursery when he was three because I needed to work. It was a desperate time and we both broke our hearts at parting.'

But the separation that work can enforce on mother and child does not mean an end to the psychic bond. Even if time is short, if the mother and child can make the most of that time together the psychic bond can be strengthened. Claire Roberts of Miranda, New South Wales is a musician. She sings in clubs and hotels five nights a week but has managed to maintain a bond with her son Matthew. 'I am usually off to work just as his dad Simon is coming home at the end of his working day. Sometimes if Simon is late I drop Matthew off at a neighbour's house just a few doors up the road. If Simon is late it's often a last-minute rush to get out of the door, and this particular day I shuffled Matt into the car. I was working at a club that night and wasn't sure if they had a restaurant or not, and so my last-minute thoughts were about getting myself some food.

'I turned to Matthew and said "Matthew – " to which he

replied, "What do you want to eat, mum?" I had him repeat it because I couldn't believe my ears. Then I told him I would just pop inside to get something and was about to add "You just wait here," when he got in first and said, "I'll just wait in the car." '

On the other side of the world, in Ontario, Canada, another working mother, Rebecca Parkes, tries to make quiet moments during the day in which she sends mental messages to her son at his creche. She told me: 'Since my son Alex was born, we've had an amazing connection. He sleeps with my husband and I, but invariably since his birth I've always awakened just before he does. Now I'm back to work (he's in a creche at my work site) whenever I have a moment I like to stop and send him a mental "I love you." The staff have commented that almost any time I call down by phone, he points and moves towards the phone, but only when it's me. When they buzz to let me in through the security door he walks over to the gate as if he knows it's me. It doesn't matter what time of day I visit, he seems to know intuitively.

'I had often thought I'd work at my psychic connection with my children, but I am so busy that I never seem to find the time. So I'm pleasantly surprised that our telepathic connection has developed effortlessly.'

I myself work at home, but with five children running about quiet moments are rare. Usually sheer exhaustion silences me at the end of the day, and one typical evening I was sitting in a shattered heap in the front room, having left the kids fighting over their tea in the dining-room at the back of the house. I remember thinking: 'The only thing in the world I would like to eat is a tub of cottage cheese.' I thought there might be one in the fridge as I'd bought some a couple of days before (in the hope of tempting my nine-year-old off her diet of mashed potatoes), but I got no further than the thought. I didn't have the energy to find out if it was still there or had been spirited away by one of the children, either to eat or do something horrible with. About a minute later the door opened. Bill, my three-year-old, came in and held out a spoon and a tub of cottage cheese. 'Here you are, mummy, cottage cheese.'

Coincidence or mind-hopping? It was certainly a more pleasant piece of telepathy than sharing his fear when he fell in the river!

Perhaps the strangest phenomena I came across concerned mothers and children sharing not concrete thoughts but the same images of their fears. In some cases the child picked up a vision from his mother, in others the mother entered into the terrors of her young child. Vivien Greene, though perhaps known to many people as the wife of the late novelist Graham Greene, is herself a woman of great insight and sensitivity. She told me the following story at her home, Grove House in Oxfordshire, where she has among other treasures her renowned collection of Victorian dolls' houses. The entire house is a delight, especially as Vivien has placed crystals in the windows so that they catch the light – throughout the year they throw rainbow patterns across the floor.

'When my son Francis was between three and four years old,' she said, 'we were living in Oxford. Francis slept in a bed with dropside cot rails on either side. One evening I was putting him to sleep when he suddenly became distressed and told me: "I don't like the little man at the bottom of my bed."'

'In a flash I saw momentarily what my son was seeing, the top half of an elf or gnome with a malevolent spiteful face, standing there. Then just as quickly the creature was gone and there were just a pile of brown blankets at the end of the bed. I moved them. "See, darling, it was just the blankets frightening you," I reassured the child.'

'He never mentioned the little man again, but for that instant I had shared my son's terrifying vision.'

In a reversal of this situation the fears of Donata Glassmeyer of Ohio were transmitted to her daughter Hope so strongly that the child conjured them up. 'I was reading Toni Morrison's novel *The Beloved*, about a black slave woman forced to kill one of her own children to save the baby from a worse fate at the hands of the slave traders. The child's ghost haunts the mother's heart and home. I only read a few chapters that night before I felt too much sympathy for the woman. Agitated, I went upstairs to lie down with Hope. I wanted to be close to her, to feel the safety of her presence while I remembered other mothers throughout history who sacrificed their precious children in the name of love.

'The next morning Hope was very agitated about a ghost being in the house. Unafraid, she checked all the cupboards and chatted endlessly about it. I realized that my preoccupation with the novel's theme had been transmitted to my little girl.

'That day we read a benign story about a friendly little ghost who eventually finds just the right home. This defused the ghost issue in our house, and I'd learned a valuable lesson about Hope's perceptive abilities.'

Frau Beatrice Meili, a member of La Leche League in Dussnang in Switzerland, had a similar experience with her daughter Annika, her third child. When Annika was four-and-a-half she was still being breast-fed twice a day. One evening Frau Meili, who usually avoided watching anything upsetting on telly, broke her usual habit and watched a film about a mass murderer. Before long she was quite distressed by it and so went to bed. The next morning she and Annika were silently breast-feeding, a ritual they used to tune themselves in to the new day. 'But my thoughts were bleak as they ran over the film I'd watched,' she said, 'and I began wondering if the front door was locked. A wave of fear began to spread over me. Suddenly Annika let go of my breast and with wide eyes said: "Mami, I am terribly afraid. Let's go down in the kitchen." I wonder how much of my feelings were transmitted directly through the act of breast-feeding?'

We live in very noisy times, being encouraged to stimulate our children with bright toys and to start teaching them almost from the moment they emerge, if not sooner – there are mothers who try to teach their children to read in the womb. The child's waking hours are filled with activities: toddler groups, child-swaps, toddler gym clubs and toddler swimming sessions, with mum driving them to and fro like a demented Road Runner. But the psychic bond operates essentially in the silence that exists after the noise has faded. Many of the mothers involved have an inner peace, and don't depend on fulfilling competitive aims though they are competent and successful in their own spheres.

Where possible, even in the busiest schedule we should try to give our children and ourselves the time and space just to be together and harmonize naturally. A walk in the woods or across a beach – or even down to the local park – can be more rewarding, both emotionally and psychically, than the most expensive, action-packed holiday.

Of course the psychic communication you have with your children can be very useful as a monitoring device. Caroline Lajoie Peterson of Cornwall, Ontario, says: 'I have three children, aged three, two, and one, and I have to rely on my sixth sense to figure out who is doing what and where. The town house I live in with the children has four floors including the basement. Most of the time I know exactly where the kids are, but once in a while one slips by me and goes on another floor and gets into mischief. This is where it gets weird: I can feel where they are. It's like an invisible umbilical cord which binds me to each child.'

So when your kids disappear and you simply haven't the energy to seek them out and your yells are falling on deaf ears, try homing in on them with your sixth sense – it may save you an unnecessary journey. Although of course in an ideal world you'd be able to project your astral body up the stairs to check and see if they were getting up to anything really bad.

5

Breaking the Time Barrier

Mothers have an uncanny knack not only of picking up when their toddler is in distress but even knowing in advance when he is heading for trouble. I'm not talking about clairvoyants who just happen to be mums, or of women who regularly predict the 3.30 at the local racecourse. I'm referring to women whose only magical powers are tied up in the protection of their young.

I could write forever about all the misfortunes that have been averted by mums taking what seemed like irrational evasive action. But stories of accidents that did *not* take place lose their point (rather like the fisherman's tale of the one that got away). The mother who does take such evasive action might often look a fool, but as one mum said to me 'I'd sooner seem wrong and know I've prevented lots of disasters.'

The alternative – to stand back and do nothing when instinct shouts at you to move – is unthinkable. You might have the satisfaction of saying afterwards: 'There – I knew that would happen,' but that would be little consolation if your child had been hurt in any way.

Animals also appear to have this precognitive instinct where their young are concerned. In *The Magical Child* (Dutton, 1977), J.C. Pearce tells of a naturalist specializing in the study of foxes who described his long-term study of a particular fox family located near a creek in a ravine. One beautiful sunny afternoon he noticed the mother doing something he had never seen a fox do. She suddenly left her burrow and kin, went up the hillside some thirty yards away and began busily digging another burrow. She then carried each of her kits up the hill to the new den. Several hours later the reason for this atypical act became clear:

although the weather remained beautiful, a flash flood caused by a cloudburst many miles upstream suddenly filled the ravine. Had the family remained where they had been they would certainly have drowned.

While accepting that humans are very different from animals I agree with James E. Peron, whom I quoted earlier as saying that if such instincts are developed in animals, surely one should expect to find them even more highly evolved in the higher life forms. Maybe the only difference is that while cubs may utter the odd yowl at being carted around by mum, the young man cub is far more devious and goes out looking for danger. Sheryl Conlon of Brisbane in Queensland, Australia, recalls an instance where she had a premonition but did not quite avert its manifestation.

'Nathan was just over two years old and a regular little terror,' said Sheryl, 'when one day we had some friends visiting. They were all downstairs in the basement playing pool, while I was upstairs organizing our meal. All of a sudden a feeling of extreme anxiety came over me, an overwhelming nervousness and tightness in my stomach, and I knew something was going to happen to Nathan. I turned and headed downstairs in a hurry, and that was when I heard my girlfriend scream.

'I ran down the rest of the stairs and someone said, "Nathan, car". That's all I heard, and of course I thought the worst. What had happened was that Nathan had climbed into our car, which was an automatic, and had knocked it out of park. I had not put the handbrake on when I had parked it earlier, and it rolled down our very steep driveway across a busy suburban street and into the garden across the road. Thankfully no damage was done to child or car. Of course Nathan was very frightened, and we clung to each other for quite a while.'

So why should Sheryl know that Nathan was in danger if she didn't know in time to prevent the accident? I warned you at the beginning of this book that there were no neat answers. No one knows why accidents happen at a particular moment, or why some end in disaster and others in a cuddle.

At least Sheryl was there to comfort her frightened child and since Nathan was not hurt it could be argued that if the accident had been prevented entirely he would not have been taught the salutary lesson that may have given him second thoughts about future dangerous pursuits. Also of course had mum not arrived with the cavalry Nathan might have panicked and dashed back across the road in front of a passing car. But again we are back in the realm of speculation.

Julie Loyd, who lives on Walden Island just off the Pacific coast of the United States, close to Canada, has had many psychic links with her children and believes that such premonitions concerning your children are a kind of rehearsal for what you'd do in a real crisis. She sees the ones that don't come true as just as valuable as those that do. 'I wonder if my panics with my children (when disaster didn't strike) were practice panics so that if something really did come up I would be armed with all the possible solutions I'd thought of in my practice panic. This is sort of like when you get the urge to slug your kid but don't because you've already worked out beforehand why you don't believe you should.'

There are no proofs from pain, least not for a mother. Most women with children will know exactly what Sheryl means when she says: 'When watching my children play, if they fall or stumble and hurt themselves it's almost like I'm feeling it too, not as a pain but as a fuzzy electrical feeling that puts me on edge for a few seconds.'

Sheryl could comfort her child and the mother fox was able to save hers. But what about those premonitions of looming disaster against which there seem to be no logical precautions?

In 1918 Elizabeth Wilson lived in a three-storey tenement house in Logie Place in Aberdeen. Her eldest child, Netta, was healthy, but she lost her second, Amy, through gastro-enteritis, which was very prevalent at that time. When her third child Edith Cavell (named after the famous 19th-century nurse) was a few weeks old, Elizabeth was carrying the baby downstairs when a woman dressed in an old-fashioned nurse's uniform met her on the stairs and held out her arms to take the baby. Shocked, Elizabeth drew the child back into her arms. The stairs were empty and there was no one in the house with her. Four days later the child was dead with gastro-enteritis. Elizabeth had nine children in all, seven of whom survived.

Why should babies and small children die, and what purpose is served by a parent's foreknowledge? These questions are unanswerable. Many of the premonitions I have received have concerned babies or children who have died. As a mother I would of course have found it easier to write a book only about the light side of the psychic bond, or about only those stories with happy endings. I don't like thinking about children dying, though I, like many parents, have faced a sudden illness, a near-accident or a heart-stopping moment when my child has been lost. The death of their child is an issue that haunts many parents, who are only too aware of how vulnerable a tiny life is. But equally, the stories of children's deaths reiterate how very precious the life of a child is, and how important its quality.

It seems that the psychic bond sometimes emerges at the death of a child, as if trying to prepare the parent to accept what is almost impossible to accept, and may be a reminder of what a gift every day with a child is. In many of these cases the bereaved parents have spoken of the child they have lost as a golden and very special being whose few years were tinged with magic.

In Third World countries parents' grief is not diminished just because of the continuing high rate of infant mortality. Parents still need to try to give some meaning to the experience. Shirley Firth, a British expert on Indian studies, told me of an Indian family for whom the child who died was seen as a gift they might otherwise not have had. The parents had had fertility problems, and so considered themselves blessed to have had a child even for a short time. The experience concerns a two-and-a-half-year-old boy in Gujarat. The parents had taken the child to the market and bought him a little packet of fried rice nibbles. Suddenly a crow swooped down and snatched the packet from his hand. His father immediately offered to buy the little boy another packet, but the child refused, saying, 'I have no need of them, Father.' The father saw this as a sign the child would die. The child became ill soon afterwards. The father then had a dream about a fight between the Mother Goddess Makarion and the God of Death over the child's life. When initially the parents had not been fertile they had prayed to Makarion for a child, and believed it was she who had given them their son. Now even the goddess could not save the child, the father believed, for he had only been given to them for a short time. Shortly after this the boy died in his sleep of diphtheria.

Ranking equally with disease as a terror for parents is the spectre of a road accident. Eileen, who now lives on the Isle of Wight, used to live in a part of northern England where there was little traffic, so at the time her premonition did not make much sense. 'I knew my eldest son Geoffrey was going to die. It was such a strong feeling, but I never told anyone because I knew they would say I was mad. I was lying in bed one night next to my husband when I suddenly woke up. I wondered what had woken me. It wasn't the children (Geoffrey was six and his sister Pamela four-and-a-half). Then I heard a voice: "Geoffrey's going to die." It is strange to think now, but I just asked, "How?" "A bus," the voice said, "he will be killed by a bus." I was terribly shaken, but it was no use waking my husband. He would just have said I was dreaming. I wet my face in the bathroom and felt a bit more calm. I tried to talk myself out of it. "There are no buses round here. The nearest bus is right down at the bottom of the main road, and we always hold his hand. He never goes anywhere where there is a lot of traffic." Some time later our young nephew came to stay. He and Geoffrey got on really well. When my mother-in-law and sister-in-law came to collect him, out of the blue my mother-in-law asked, "Can Geoffrey come back with us?" He had never been away from me and I didn't want him to go, but Geoffrey really wanted to. He was a very brave little chap. I had always felt Geoffrey didn't belong to me; he was somehow different.

'Pamela was very outgoing, but Geoffrey was always so sensitive. I just used to want to throw my arms round him and keep him safe. When he was born and put into my arms, he started to suck his thumb. "Isn't he beautiful!" everyone said, and he was. He would lie in his little cot at the bottom of my bed with his eyes wide open as if he knew all the secrets of the world, and the nurse said he had been here before.

'I was so frightened when my mother-in-law wanted him to go, because she lived in the town, but I couldn't explain about the bus. She would have thought I was mad. "Go on," my mother-in-law said to Geoffrey, "say goodbye to your mother." I didn't want him to say the words. I felt so strange, but I couldn't say anything except "Cheerio."

'He went on the Sunday night. We weren't on the phone, nor were they. On the Thursday my husband said, "Go and bring him back. The house is like a morgue without him." So I went but he was enjoying himself at his gran's so much that he wanted to stay till Sunday, so I went home without him.

'On the Saturday Pam and I went to my mother-in-law's house. We were sitting at the table having lunch while Geoffrey was getting ready to go out with his gran and my sister-in-law and nephew. I didn't know what to do as his gran was looking after him, but I didn't want him to go. I wanted to get him home. I had bought him a t-shirt to wear and put it on him. "Let me fix it," I said, and he stood next to me quite quietly. Then they all went out. I was sitting in a chair by the fire. I thought, "I musn't look down the yard and watch him go," because I suddenly remembered I'd seen a film where a woman watched someone go and they never came back. Then Pam and I left to make our way home, stopping at the shops nearby to get some fruit to make pies with when we got home. I said I'd come back on Sunday for Geoffrey. Geoffrey had asked for a cowboy outfit for his birthday in five weeks' time. I looked at a cowboy hat in a shop window – should I get it? I stood for ages looking at the hat, but then decided not to buy it. I crossed over the road to where a man was selling goods on a piece of waste land. Should I get a couple of notebooks for the kids? Again I hesitated for ages. I just couldn't buy anything for him.

'As I passed the end of my mother-in-law's street I saw a bus parked there. "Geoffrey, the bus," I cried out. "Oh, no," Pam said, "Where's Geoffrey?" because she couldn't see him. I tried to laugh it off for Pam's sake. I wanted to go to my mother-in-law's house but I'd got no excuse. I wanted to know he was all right but I knew she'd say I was fussing. It was the football season and special buses often brought people to the match, so it wasn't strange to see one there, I reasoned.

'I knew but I still went home. There was nothing else to do.'

Pam is now in her thirties. Though she was only four-and-a-half at the time she can still remember the incident. 'We had been looking at colouring books in the market. Then out of the blue mum cried out, "Geoffrey, the bus." Mum tried to laugh it off but she went quite white.'

'When I got home,' Eileen said, 'I was cooking the dinner when my husband, who was a policeman, arrived home. "Who was in the car with you?" I asked him. "Just a policeman," he replied. He went up to the bathroom. I followed him. "Geoffrey's had an accident," he said, "he was knocked down by a car." "Is he dead?" I asked. "No," replied my husband, "but he's hurt his head." "It wasn't a car," I said, "it was a bus." "How could you possibly know that?" he asked. "I saw the bus parked on the corner of your mother's road," I told him.

'He hadn't wanted to tell me it was a bus because he thought it would frighten me even more. Geoffrey was such a little lad, and buses are so big.

'My husband took me to the hospital ward. I knew Geoffrey would die. The voice had told me. I saw a child half-sitting up in bed. At first I thought it was Geoffrey and said to myself, "It can't be that bad if he's sitting up. Maybe the voice was wrong." But then I saw Geoffrey. He had tubes sticking out everywhere. "Will he be all right?" I asked the doctor.

'The doctor just ignored me, saying to my husband, "You know what it's like. You see these things with head injuries." She was so hard. After that I couldn't bear to stay. They said he would recover, but they didn't know what I knew. "If he comes out of the coma," my husband told me, "I'll arrange for someone to get you back to hospital. If anything happens, I'll come home." My brother-in-law was at the house when we got back. "Geoffrey's got a good skull," he said, "He'll come out of it." I said nothing.

'I was making toast when a car drew up. "It's only Bill," said my brother-in-law, "he'll be coming to tell us Geoffrey's on the mend." The accident had happened at 3.45 that afternoon. Geoffrey died at 11.30 that night. He never regained consciousness.

'I still can't understand the voice. People say it was God speaking to me, but how can they be so sure? I tried to sort it out in my head. Was it something from Geoffrey's mind? Whose voice was it? Was it someone who had passed on, trying to prepare me? If I hadn't stopped so long looking at the cowboy hat and the notebooks, I would have witnessed the accident. Was it planned that way? Was it all meant to happen for some purpose? I don't know.'

Enid, who lives in the south of England, was ironing and only half-watching television when a programme about childhood leukaemia came on. She looked across at her lively three-year-old daughter sitting by the window and thought, 'How would I cope if she got leukaemia?'

'I knew at that moment I was going to lose her very soon. I'd seen programmes on childhood deaths before, and though like any mum they struck fear in my heart, this was different. Six months later my little girl had died of leukaemia. She was only ill for a few weeks. Though it was many, many years ago I can still see her sitting by that window and me doing the ironing.'

Eileen and Enid might ask: 'What is the point of a premonition if you cannot do anything to prevent the outcome?' Who can say for sure? But it would seem that at least sometimes a premonition gives you a fighting chance to save your child. Even if you lose you may in some way have been given an opportunity to make the most of those last days – or even minutes – that you can spend with your child and express the love that might otherwise get lost along the way. We have all at some time sent a child to bed crying – they can all be little devils at times. But even in those moments of pain and frustration we have to remember how precious they are. In some ways the proximity of death can be a helpful reminder of our priorities.

Certainly Enid took comfort from the forewarning, and felt her remaining time with her daughter was doubly precious. As her daughter lay dying Enid was heavily pregnant. Peter arrived later than scheduled, the day after she lost her precious daughter. 'I believe Peter waited to be born to show me there is life and hope,' she told me. Peter is now grown up, and from the day of his birth has been a constant joy to her.

Mercifully few of us will have a premonition that we will lose our child. For those of us who have fit, well and even at times annoying children, such warnings can be a reminder of how precious they are and how little the rest really matters. Enjoy each day with your child – leave the housework, don't worry if you're not as efficient in the working world as you were before. Your child is the greatest gift, the most important career in the world. Even though they will probably outlive you, you lose your children in all sorts of natural ways as they grow up, so enjoy them while they are close to you.

The psychic bond is made up of love and hope. The premonitions concerning mothers and children can bring hope of future happiness as well as sorrow, as Maura Sesin of Mexico found. 'My second son Omar, who is eight years old, has a special power to know the future. When he foretells something he becomes very serious even though he is little; he has a different tone in his voice, a tone that a child doesn't usually use.

'I had lost two babies, which had left me in a terrible depression. I was in bed and Omar, then four years old, came and stood by my side talking and playing. Suddenly he said very seriously and with that special tone in his voice, "When my brother is twelve years old and I am seven years old you will get pregnant again, and this time we will have a baby." Before this came to pass I lost another baby and also lost all hope of having another. My husband and I decided that we would not try again. Yet, in January, 1990 I got pregnant again – my son Rodrigo was twelve and Omar seven. This time my baby was healthy, and he is now four months old. Throughout this pregnancy I bled, as I had in the previous ones, so I told my sons not to get excited about the baby and to be prepared not to have him. Omar looked at me straight in the eye and said loud, clear and sure, "This baby will be born." Indeed, it happened as he said.'

Omar's case opens up a whole new field of exploration, for once a child can talk premonitions become a two-way affair. We cannot know if children can see into the future even before they can speak of it, but we do know that once they can speak most of their premonitions do not concern far-flung events but rather those people and places closest to them.

Nearly 50 years on Elspeth can still remember how a premonition enabled her to save her mother's life. 'During the Second World War, when I was about five, my family were living in Portland. Dad was in the Merchant Navy – he was a salvage diver – and Mum decided that we would stay where he was based so we wouldn't be separated. Mum and I were walking along the beach with our dog, Blue. I can remember him now. "Quick, Mum," I suddenly shouted, "there's a bad plane coming." "No there isn't, love," she reassured me, looking up at the sky. But I grabbed her and called the dog and we all three ran behind a rock. Mum went along with it to humour me. Seconds later a bomb was dropped on the beach a bit ahead of where we were walking. I hadn't heard anything, I just knew it was there.'

The protective instinct of mothers is well-documented though little understood, especially when it depends on an advance warning system that would be the envy of any Defence Ministry. Yet as we've seen children's protective instincts can be just as fierce. In Elspeth's case her foreknowledge saved their lives. When a child has a sudden, apparently irrational fear, it's as well to heed it.

For example, one little girl warned her dad not to accompany her and her mother on a walk. He thought she was just being difficult, but while on the walk he tripped over a branch and hurt his leg. 'I told you not to come, Dad,' his daughter said wisely.

Cath from Glastonbury was surprised by the psychic and spiritual awareness of her young son, Dom. She was never afraid of his gifts, however, and indeed took what he said very seriously. On one occasion his foreknowledge prevented what might have been a nasty accident. She told me: 'I have always wondered at Dom's wisdom, and have learned to listen to him. Once when he was quite little we were in the car when he told me to slow right down. Almost immediately a car pulled out in front of me.'

So what do all these experiences have to say to us? First that if we get a seemingly illogical feeling of danger about letting our child go somewhere or do something we should nevertheless heed it. Of course if you are constantly issuing warnings or prohibitions then your child will come to ignore you. But if you keep the negative instructions to a minimum then your child will know when you are serious. Second, if your child warns you about something, take the warning seriously. There is much we don't know about children, but they should always be respected.

6

Before Childbirth

Joseph and Mary were walking through the wood,
They saw cherries and ripe berries, as red as any blood.
Joseph and Mary walked through a garden green,
They saw cherries and ripe berries, the finest ever seen.
Then up spoke Virgin Mary, so meek and so mild,
Saying: 'Pluck me cherries, Joseph, for I am with child.'
Then Joseph flew in anger, in anger so wild,
Saying: 'Let him pluck thee cherries, who got thee with child.'
Then up spake baby Jesus from within his mother's womb,
Saying: 'Bow down, you cherry tree, and give my mother some.'
Then the cherry tree bowed down unto Mary's hand,
She said: 'Joseph, I have cherries unto my command.'

The Cherry Tree Carol

This old English folk song tells of a very special baby talking to his mother while still in the womb. But is it possible for mere mortal children to communicate from within? Many mothers would say yes. In pregnancy, and in some cases even before, they feel they have been in contact with their unborn children. Up to a point they have the support of Professor Peter Hepper of the School of Psychology at the Queen's University of Belfast, who has studied pre-natal learning extensively. He found that the babies of women who had regularly watched the television soap opera *Neighbours* while pregnant responded to the theme tune after they were born. Indeed, Cathy Critchley of Essex told me: 'During the last month of my second pregnancy I noticed how the baby inside me would react to familiar telly signature tunes (kicking furiously and moving excitedly). Three such tunes were those for the *News at One*, *Neighbours* and *EastEnders*. After the birth of my daughter I was constantly amazed at her reactions almost from birth (and lasting until the age of four or five months) to hearing these familiar signature tunes. She would jerk her head towards the telly as soon as the tune started; she would stop feeding and turn her whole body towards the source of the sound.

'It was certainly evidence that babies hear and remember pre-birth sounds,' Cathy said, 'I only wish I had introduced her to something a bit more classical!'

Professor Hepper explained: 'Recognition is undoubtedly based on hearing, and in all probability requires the storing of highly specific patterns of sound. Babies tested only responded to the *Neighbours* theme and not any other tune, nor the *Neighbours* tune played backwards. We have demonstrated learning as early as 24 weeks (in fact other research has suggested that the *Neighbours* tune soothed foetuses as young as 12 weeks old.) It is unlikely to be psychic communication between mother and foetus, mainly because it is difficult to see how this would occur.

'There is undoubtedly some communication between mother and baby, as there is much evidence that a baby responds to the mother or anyone else pushing on the abdomen by pushing back. Exactly what the foetus feels or gets from this is unknown, but this certainly stimulates the mother into action and believing she is interacting with her foetus.'

Cathy's is a simple case and explainable in terms of known science. Does this inevitably rule out any possibility of a psychic connection? Let's take a look at the more complex case of Felicity, who lives in the Home Counties.

Felicity is now in her 50s and her daughter is 15, but before this child was born she picked up information about her that even the most sophisticated of today's scans could not record. She used to talk to her unborn child, especially about her own father and older brother. 'Gradually I realized the baby was returning the communication and was talking to me in my mind,' she said. It was as if Felicity had heard the baby's voice, and eventually conversations took place. 'When I was about six months pregnant I asked the baby if she was healthy, and she said she was.

' "Any blemishes?" I asked her. It might seem daft to ask that when she said she'd already said she was healthy, but first-time mums especially want everything about the baby to be perfect. "Well," the baby told me, "I do have a birthmark on my heel that is shaped like an apple."

'When the baby was born she was absolutely perfect except for an apple-shaped mark on one of her heels. There were no such marks in the history of our family.'

For Diane Jardel of Dorset the communication was one way, but the reassuring messages she received from her child helped her through a difficult labour. 'I had been in hospital eight weeks earlier than my due date because I kept getting contractions, and had been put on a drip to stop them. I was also increasingly weak and anxious about my baby, as I had a fibroid growing alongside it and had developed a chest infection which had been treated with large doses of antibiotics. One evening just as I was falling asleep I "saw" two large brown eyes looking at me calmly and happily, and heard a voice telling me that everything was all right. I knew that it was my baby talking to me, and I immediately felt relieved and calm.

'When he was born six weeks prematurely he was in good health except for a long-lasting jaundice, and I felt a very strong bond with him though he stayed in an incubator for four weeks.'

This situation was very different from that of a mother 'interpreting' and giving meaning to her child's kicks and movements. We can't really separate mother from foetus, though it is perhaps more comfortable to accept that it is all in the mother's mind.

An even more dramatic instance of pre-birth communication comes from Lisa, mother of one of the youngest heart-transplant children in Britain. She told me how almost from the time Erica was conceived she was convinced in spite of medical reassurances that there was something seriously wrong with her unborn child. 'Before my eldest daughter Fiona was born everything felt fine and I didn't worry at all, so I knew it wasn't an ordinary pregnancy anxiety I was experiencing about Erica. From early on in the pregnancy I felt really bad about things. I kept having terrifying thoughts that the baby I was carrying had something dreadfully wrong with her, though I couldn't have told you exactly what. As the pregnancy developed I felt worse though clinically everything was OK. I had one of those urine tests and there was protein in it, so the doctors wondered if the baby had spina bifida. More detailed tests showed she was absolutely fine.

'I thought perhaps that that had been what was worrying me, and for a couple of days I was fine. But then the feeling came back as bad as before. I was even organizing in my mind how to bury the baby. I knew she would be born but knew I couldn't keep her. It was really strange. We had recently moved to a new area, and I kept thinking how I wanted to go back to my old home town for the funeral since all my friends and relations were there. I used to think like this right up to the end of the pregnancy. I never planned for her as I did with Fiona. I thought, "I'll wait till later. What's the point in making any plans?"

'Then suddenly one day towards the end of the pregnancy I had a burning desire to get Erica's room ready. I hadn't felt the same urgency with Fiona. For her the preparations had carried on steadily throughout the pregnancy. But with Erica I had to get the room ready straight away, though I never thought she'd sleep in it. It was an ordinary natural labour, and Erica weighed eight and three quarter pounds. I said to my husband Gerald, "Is she all right?" and he said she was. She had a bit of trouble breathing at first but Gerald didn't tell me. I knew nothing about it till much later. When we were on the ward I inspected her and saw her feet were turned inwards. I pointed this out to the paediatrician, who said he'd get the consultant to have a look but that I shouldn't worry. The next morning the consultant came and said Erica's feet were fine and that it was purely a positional thing and that she would just need a bit of manipulation to put it right. I thought, "OK. That's it sorted out. That was what was worrying me when I was pregnant." But inside I knew that was not it. There was still something more.

'For the next three to three-and-a-half weeks the feeling was still there. Of course I was delighted with Erica and very happy, but it was as if there was a big cloud hanging over us. I looked at her and inspected her all over. She was big and bonny, but I said to Gerald: "She's got a funny shaped chest. She's pigeon-chested." He said: "Fancy a little girl being pigeon-chested," and left it at that, but I was still dreadfully worried there was something very wrong. At four weeks I started to pick up clear signs that she wasn't right. I trotted off to the doctor on several occasions; he would listen to her chest and say everything was fine and send us home. He thought I was fussing, but I hadn't fussed with Fiona. At the sixth-week check I said I thought she was having difficulty breathing. The doctor said he thought he could hear something, but then said it was all right. He said I could always see my GP if I was worried at any time. The following Friday she wouldn't take her two o'clock feed. I said to Gerald, "If she doesn't take her six o'clock feed I shall call the emergency doctor." She did refuse her next feed, and I called the doctor. He came out and pronounced her fine. I was very het up because she wasn't feeding and I was worried she would get dehydrated. I insisted I wanted her to have a chest X-ray because she was coughing. "If it will make you feel better," he said, "you can take her for a chest X-ray at the local hospital to set your mind at rest." I took her straight to hospital.

'When we got there the doctor realized something was wrong, gave her an X-ray and called a consultant. Erica was in severe heart failure and was sent straight up to the ward. On the ward she was put into an oxygen tent and was wired up to a heart monitor. Five weeks later she was given a heart transplant. For a long time afterwards, even when she was well, every day was a bonus. We didn't worry about the little things any more. I was too frightened to think about the future. Only now over two years later can I feel more confident and accept that she is mine.'

Lisa's case is not meant to encourage you to go against medical opinion, which would be very unwise. But it is important (though often very difficult) for expectant mothers to have the confidence to follow their own inner voice or that of their unborn child and use this to express the intuitions that can supplement medical knowledge. In extreme cases where there is no clear-cut right or wrong a mother's instincts are ultimately perhaps the ones to follow. Women do know their own child best, even before he is born, and increasingly midwives and health visitors are recognizing the expertise of the expectant or new mother.

Even when the mother herself has professional medical training it can be her sixth sense that predominates. Rita Laws gave me this account of Andrea, a friend of hers and a midwife: 'During her pregnancy Andrea became agitated about her unborn baby's health. Despite reassurances from a midwife and an obstetrician, Andrea, herself a midwife, continued to insist that something was wrong. Her child was in grave danger. Even when an ultrasound scan showed her baby to be healthy, her uneasiness persisted. The labour was long but normal, and Andrea gave birth to a beautiful baby boy who was very much alive. The umbilical cord, however, had two true knots in it. Had they been tighter the baby would have been deprived of oxygen and probably stillborn.'

True knots are quite rare in umbilical cords. The child was born healthy, but it was an instance no one could have foreseen – yet Andrea did 'see' it.

Midwives, who are so close to the practicalities of pregnancy, can become bound up in the 'magic' (in the paranormal sense of the word) of birth. When I spoke about women's birth experiences to the now deceased Sir Alec Turnbull, then professor of the Nuffield Department of Obstetrics and

Gynaecology of the John Radcliffe Hospital at Oxford, he said he had not really encountered such things but added that mothers were unlikely to confide in him or the other obstetricians; they would be much more likely to talk to the midwives, who were after all in the front lines with them.

Megan, a midwife with ten years experience, told me: 'I was driving home after taking an antenatal clinic but couldn't get one woman out of my mind. The baby was the right size for the dates and neither the doctor nor I had detected any problems. But I had a feeling something was wrong. I drove straight to her house, though I was quite tired, and asked if I could have another feel of her tummy. She wasn't surprised to see me, and admitted she was herself worried though she couldn't put her finger on the reason. I decided to get her a scan as soon as possible, so I rang the consultant. He was very sympathetic as he knew I don't normally fuss, and the woman was given a scan the next day, though there was no apparent reason for us to be worried. The scan showed that the baby had developed hydrocephalus. The infant was delivered early by Caesarean that day and the fluid drained off. Because of the timely intervention he is now a normal, healthy little boy.'

Maria Cadaxa of Tucson, Arizona, writes: 'As a midwife and mother of four I have been intrigued by the definite super-sensory link between mothers and their children, especially infants. Regarding pre-natal links I have yet to come across a mother totally surprised by her baby's gender. Nine out of ten had a definite knowing or a very strong suspicion. I believe this "knowing" has a physical and spiritual component, on the one hand the mother's body recognizing the new hormones controlling her body and on the other the connection she has with her child's spirit.

'Dreams are often prophetic, both as to gender and appearance. For example, a mother considering an abortion may have a very clear dream in which a child with dark, curly hair appears and asks to stay. She consents – the child who is subsequently born is a girl with dark, curly hair.'

The woman may know the gender but might not necessarily want to share this information, as Joan Cannon of New South Wales told me. 'Jode is five months old, and most times knows easily when to communicate with me,' she said. 'I guess I knew he was a boy about five months into my pregnancy. We both wanted a girl, and I tried so hard to convince both myself and my husband that it was. Yet I always referred to the baby as "he" or "him". I'd lie in bed with my husband at night saying, "I'm sure it's a girl," then before I went to sleep I'd laugh to myself and rub my belly because I knew he was a boy.

'My labour was very short (thirty minutes after arriving at hospital), though even so all I could think of after he was born was "Thank God the pain's over." Nobody told me he was a boy; they didn't have to. I seemed to know exactly what he expected of me. We spent the first two days just staring at each other, sort of getting into each other's minds. I came home four days later and it was like we'd known each other forever. It all felt so natural, though he was my first.'

Tracey Nelson of Redhead, Australia, said: 'My dreams have never come true in real life, except for the two concerning my unborn children. With my first pregnancy I dreamed three times that my baby would be a boy, blond, born two months early and perfectly all right. While awake I told myself not even to think about this, as babies two months' premature aren't always "perfectly all right". Yet Simon was born at 33 weeks, and was blond and healthy.

'Before I even knew I was pregnant the second time I dreamed that I had twin girls called Jill and Sarah. Later in the pregnancy I was looking at some pottery "babies" and kept being strongly drawn to the twins. At 14 weeks gestation twins were diagnosed, and I said they would be two girls. Sure enough we now have Beth and Sarah (my husband doesn't like the name Jill).'

Tracey's first dream prepared her for an early baby. Many women have told me they have known they would have an early baby even when their other children have been full-term, and it would seem this is almost a safety mechanism to insulate the mother from shock so she is ready to cope. Although ancient cultures put great store on the importance of divining the future from dreams (remember Joseph and his 'technicolour dreamcoat') Tracey, like many other women, found that when not pregnant her dreams were inaccurate. I believe these special dreams are part of a woman's heightened intuition or sixth sense during pregnancy and childbirth. A pregnant woman is less in touch with the material world and so less resistant to outside influences and 'common sense' which might otherwise keep her from acknowledging the validity of her instincts. Those who are pregnant or in constant communion with small children do find that dreams are just one element of the whole battery of visions, apparently random associations, unbidden thoughts and fantasies that flip between mother and foetus or mother and child, which if accepted and used are valuable indicators of the unseen and unknown. Freud called dreams the 'royal road to the unconscious', but he did not study the maternal shortcut across fields still unexplored by science.

After the birth, the dreamy states of pregnancy are replaced by the half-sleeping states of sitting by a sick or restless child through the midnight hours. If you've got the energy, grab a pen and paper and jot down a few of your thoughts or semi-dreams at these times. If not, don't worry, for this is a land of magic and unreality you will inhabit for many years, even as you doze by the fire waiting for your teenager's key to turn in the lock. Psychic phenomena, ESP – the terms come thick and fast, as do 'explanations' – but as you watch away the small hours you just stare into these untapped dimensions and accept.

The prophetic dreams of pregnancy helped another mother to reconcile herself to the birth of a boy which at first she did not really want. Karin Liedtke was living in San Francisco when they started. 'I had wanted to have a child all my life, but things were never right enough and the older I became the less prepared I felt to embark on the responsibility. By the time I was 27, though, I felt so biologically ready that it seemed somehow everything would fall into place.

'While I had wanted a child, it had always been a girl I envisioned. A few months before I became pregnant my husband I discussed planning to try and conceive a child in a year or so. He asked what I would do if I had a boy, and I realized I was not completely open to the idea. I then started to have dreams, three of them over about three months' time, in which I had a boy. In these dreams he was newborn to age six. In each dream I loved him very much, and upon awakening felt there was no reason not to be joyful about having a boy.

'A month after the last dream I conceived, a year ahead of schedule. I knew it was a boy and Rob felt it was a boy too. Once Rory was born I was delighted with him. I adore him. It seemed I had to be more open and realize I would love whomever I bore – then this being came to us. Now it seems utterly silly that I ever had reservations to begin with.'

Since writing her experience, Karin has had many hardships to face, marital break-up, relocation and the need to work full-time outside her own field of holistic health. She spends less time than she would wish with her beloved son. But the bond forged before Rory was conceived has endured, and she says: 'My life is coming together again and I feel great.'

Premonitions in dreams have brought both sorrow and joy to Karla Colon, who now lives in New Orleans. Her story also gave me the chance to test one of Karla's premonitions for myself, but it was not an easy time: at stake was the life of one of Karla's children.

When her first child was conceived Karla was living in Puerto Rico with her husband, and had recurring dreams that she had lost her baby in a grocery store. 'I could not speak enough Spanish to get anyone to help me. After these dreams, I can't really explain how, but I knew that the baby would not be born. Many friends and family wanted to give me gifts for the child but

I asked them to please wait till the baby was born. At 20 weeks I had an ultrasound scan. There we discovered that our little boy would not live.

'During my next pregnancy I knew again that this baby was not to be. I had had several dreams that she was a girl and that I lost her while swimming. Again I asked people to wait before bringing their gifts. My family and friends tried to tell me I was just anxious because I had lost the other baby, but I knew that I was just going through the motions. On 23rd May, 1989 I delivered a baby girl at 23 weeks.' The child did not survive.

It was during her third pregnancy that Karla wrote to me, on 11 May, 1991: 'At six weeks I had a dream that my doctor told me I was having twins. But when I told him I was expecting twins he just laughed. Later at my scheduled ultrasound test I told the technician about the dream. She smiled and left to go and get the radiologist, who then confirmed I was bearing twins.

'Prior to my twentieth week, I had another of many dreams of having identical boys. When the doctor asked during another ultrasound test if I wanted to know what sex they were I told him they were boys, and I was right. My husband and I are in the process of divorce, but I feel so good and so positive about this pregnancy. This time everyone else wants to wait to bring the children gifts until they are born, but I've been telling them it's OK this time.'

Karla's twins were indeed born fit and well, but she has told me of one other premonition: 'I have had a few bad feelings about the baby on the right side. In one dream I pick up his brother and tell him, "Let's go save your brother." I hope I am wrong and that he is OK. All the tests point to him being OK.'

In June 1991 Karla wrote to me again enclosing a picture of two delightful babies: Richard, who weighed 6 lbs 6 oz, and Matthew, who was just over 6 lbs. But her last premonition had been accurate. As she had dreamed, Matthew got into trouble during labour so that she had to have an emergency Caesarean section. Now the babies are home and healthy.

A mother's instincts can help out even before conception. Jenny was having problems getting pregnant. 'After two years of trying for a child, I was getting so anxious that the doctor told me my anxiety was probably why I could not conceive. Then at home one weekend I suddenly had this strange, overwhelmingly powerful vision – it was fantastic. I could see myself at my mother-in-law's house holding my own baby and chatting away. A feeling of certainty and calm came over me, and even when the moment passed it left me changed and so happy. I stopped worrying. Within the next month I had conceived.'

Regina Paleau of Staten Island, New York, also knew that she had become pregnant, though doctors insisted she couldn't possibly tell. 'My husband and I had been trying to conceive for about two years. I had even started to take my temperature with a Basil thermometer to pinpoint ovulation. I wasn't worried, however, I knew when our baby was ready to come it would happen. One night we made love quite impulsively. The next night I dreamed I was pregnant with a big rounded belly and friends surrounding me asking me how I felt. I told them I was elated.

'From that point on I "knew" I was pregnant, although it would be weeks before I could confirm it with a test. I went to be tested when my menstrual period was five days late, and the doctor suggested this could be an hysterical pregnancy. I knew it was not because that dream had been so true for me, and of course I was pregnant and had conceived the night before the dream.'

It may be in cases that where anxiety is a factor blocking pregnancy such premonitions can ease the way by instilling confidence in the parents-to-be. Medical science is starting to recognize this, and in 1989 doctors at the London Hospital began looking at folk remedies in some cases.

The anthropologist Dr Sue Jennings and her team offered prospective parents who were facing difficulties courses in mask-making, dance and drama. Dr Jennings prescribed dancing to

Indian music or African drums as good therapy, because the patients relax instead of worrying about the 'technical side' of conception. She denied this was an idea alien to Western culture, pointing to ancient fertility rites in Britain such as Maypole and Morris dancing.

Once conception has been achieved, the psychic link can be used in cases where conventional social therapies fail to help mothers-to-be come to terms with the needs of their unborn child. This link has been studied by Rosalie Denenfeld, who lives in Harper Woods, Michigan and is the mother of two children. Her thesis studying the relationship between first-time mothers and their unborn child was produced as part of her graduate degree in humanistic and clinical psychology at the Center for Humanistic Studies in 1984. She sees the most important implication of her work as helping mothers in disadvantaged circumstances, especially teenage mothers, to become aware of a pre-natal bond, not just physically but emotionally and spiritually, so that they may be more willing to change their harmful lifestyle that can be threatening the foetus, and also perhaps break out of the cycle of abuse that was reflected in their own lives.

Rosalie worked with ten first-time mothers, using such techniques as focusing to discover deep levels of awareness within the body through intuitive means, keeping a journal, interviewing, art and music. The women were well-educated, middle-class and married, and were experiencing a minimum amount of internal, family and social conflicts due to their pregnancies. She comments that their 'impressively clear verbal descriptions and artistic expressions provided a rich introduction to how pregnant women may experience relating to their unborn child'.

Rosalie says: 'A woman who is pregnant for the first time seems to experience her relationship with her unborn child as a catalyst for personal expansion and increased capacity for love. Because of the uniquely intimate physical unity between the pregnant woman and her unborn child, there may exist a peak potential for interaction on a physical, emotional and spiritual level.' She discovered that as the attachment was increased by the love that grows between mother and unborn child, so the fear of the unknown, that is greatest with the first birth than with any subsequent ones, diminishes.

On the spiritual level, Rosalie points out that for a woman, 'other than experiencing nine months in her own mother's womb, pregnancy is the only time she has the opportunity to experience a dramatic contrast to the separateness to which each of us is subject. Pregnancy is the ultimate intimacy possible between human beings. Pregnancy may be a vehicle meant to awaken love within women and bring more love into the world.'

Some of the women Rosalie studied found their bodies picking up their unborn babies' feelings. Gail explained: 'Every once in a while I have a feeling but I don't know where it comes from. And then I realize that I am not the one having the feeling.'

The first time Gail experienced this was during a thunderstorm. 'We live on a hilltop and our bedroom has two great big windows. There are trees right outside the window so it is almost like you are outside. When there are storms, it seems like it comes right into the room. One night I woke up feeling really afraid. There was all this lightning and noise. I personally really love storms, I love to hear the thunder and see the lightning. But I woke up and was really afraid. I got out of bed and walked round the house. I couldn't figure it out, and suddenly I realized I wasn't the one who was afraid; it was the unborn baby. So I talked to it. I told it that it was a storm and that it was the noise that was probably disturbing but that it was OK. The fear went away.'

Communication with the unborn infant seems to serve a number of important purposes. It can warn or reassure the mother of medical complications or an early birth. And it can help the mother come to terms with the sometimes frightening responsibility of creating another human being. I am not advocating completely disregarding doctors, but there is a lot to be said for listening to your own intuition about the well-being of your unborn child. Do not be surprised that you are in tune with your child, because after all it is part of your body and the link is not just physical.

The mother-to-be can get to know the baby in her womb. Much has been written about this, but the most important thing to remember is to choose a way that makes you feel comfortable. Once again, follow your instincts. Some women find specific techniques useful, but there appear to be no rights and wrongs. You will know the best course to take if you just listen to yourself.

One word of caution, however: You are experiencing for two, as Ann of British Columbia found out. A very different kind of foetal monitoring was at work when an evening of passion turned out not to be the closely guarded secret she had imagined. 'When I was seven months pregnant with my second child my lover and I made love one night in his lorry. Though it may sound sleazy to some, this particular incident was a warm and happy memory for me, one where I felt adventurous but also close and friendly to the man involved.

'When my son (the baby she was pregnant with at the time) was three years old, we were passing a parked lorry one day. "That's a mummy lorry," my son announced. Humouring him, I asked, "Are there daddy lorries, too?" Ignoring my question, he said, "You were in a mummy lorry. You had no clothes on."

'Well, the only time I'd been in a lorry with no clothes on was that one night. Maybe babies can project their astral bodies outside the womb and spy on what their mothers are doing, or it could be a case of telepathy. After all, when a baby is inside it is very intimately linked with your physical system, and perhaps with your thoughts and emotions as well.'

7

Have They Been Here Before?

Nurses sometimes say of a very alert newborn baby, 'Oh, he's been here before!' The acceptable reply from a mother is 'Do you think so?' It is perhaps not wise to answer: 'I know, he was my son before in a previous life.' But some women do believe they have known their children from previous incarnations, and that the birth is a reunion of sorts. This is perhaps the most intriguing aspect of the mother and child bond, and one that confirms for some women their link with their child.

Cath believes that the bond between herself and her son Dom stems from a previous life together. 'At his birth there was immediate recognition between us; I knew him. I loved him and I realized he was an old soul. When he was a baby he used to wake up a lot but he never cried. I used to get an image of his eyes, and into my head would come "Dom needs me" – so I would leave what I was doing and go to him, and he would be waiting.

'He has the same dreams as me, picks up on my worries and reads my thoughts. I do not know whether he picks up on my dreams or I on his. When I asked him how he always knew what I was thinking he told me, "It's easy. I just read the pictures in your mind." '

Tantalizing hints that Dom may have lived before came when Dom was about two-and-a-half. 'He climbed on a friend's motor bike and started to rev it up. "I know how to do this," he said, "I was a biker. I was killed in a crash." It wasn't like a little boy playing or talking. He only mentioned it once more.'

Reincarnation is a basic tenet of the Hindu religion. The idea that a dead relative may be seeking to return as a new child is something to be welcomed, as this account by Eleanor Nisbett of the University of Warwick shows. She visited a Punjabi Hindu woman who was then in her mid-30s. This woman had been brought up in Delhi but was living in the West Midlands.

'On the wall was a photograph of her late father-in-law, garlanded with sandalwood. Sultanas were stuck to the part of the glass frame that was over his mouth. Every day she offered him *prashad* (food offered in worship) after "doing jay" (worshipping the goddess and offering her sultanas). I asked why she did this, as his spirit had probably already taken a new body. She said that by offering him prashad daily she was showing him her respect. After all, if he were alive she would be feeding him. Then she added that yes, he had probably come back again, as her eldest son.

'After having two daughters she had fallen pregnant again within a few months, and had decided to have an abortion as there was no one to help her cope with three babies. The night before she went for the abortion, her late father-in-law (whom she had never met) appeared to her in a dream and told her he would be taking birth in her son. So she did not terminate the pregnancy. When she took her son to India all the relatives remarked that he was exactly like her father-in-law.'

But the belief in reincarnation is not confined to the East. Rozanne Silverwood of Lewes, Delaware, believes her special bond with her daughter Margaret started not when she was born or even before but with the death of her husband Mark's grandmother, Margaret (who was known to the family as Nan). When she and Mark went to the wake, Rozanne 'sensed a tingling that started at my shoulders and went down my spine. I knew she was standing behind me.

'At the funeral the next day I felt as though my heart would break. I had a physical throbbing that would not ease up. I wondered at myself: after all, I did not know this woman well enough to be as troubled as I was. After the funeral we walked towards the middle of the town where her old house stood. As we walked I felt her presence beside us. My spirit reached towards hers to make a feeble attempt at comforting her.

'Over the next few months I discovered that our paths were fused together that day in a very special way. One evening when we were out to dinner we drank a toast to her memory, and in doing so seemed to invoke her presence with such force that we commented on it at the same time.

'Mark said, "You know I think that Nan will be joining us soon. I know this sounds crazy, but I think she wants to come back into physical form. In fact I think she wants to come as our child." I was aghast. After all, we had never come this close to talking about having children, much less discussing the idea of conceiving an old relative!

'Periodically I would check to see if this being we called Nan was still around. There were still many doubts in my mind about this whole arrangement, but each time I would make an attempt to contact her I felt a strong sense of her presence and a soft smile growing inside of me.

'The day that we decided we were ready to begin trying to conceive a child I was both excited and scared to death. Mark was mostly scared to death. But as we talked we felt the sureness of our instincts by the eager presence of the being we were preparing a place for.

'The night before I took the pregnancy test I had a dream I was standing with many people on the banks of a river. Tugging at my leg was a little girl. She looked dark-skinned, like a Latin American. She had to leave and go through a door rather than take the bridge to get to the other side of the river. She said her name was Consuela and she said goodbye to me with her happy eyes. I made an attempt at remembering my school Spanish and said "Poquito minuto". What I meant was "I will see you in a very little while."

'That morning I took the test and it was positive. That weekend we visited St Patrick's Cathedral in New York with Mark's parents. At the shrine of St Margaret we started to talk about Nan. I asked Mark's mother what Margaret's confirmation name had been, and she told me it was Consuela.

'As the baby grew so did my worries. I decided to have an alphafeta protein test at 16 weeks, and a week later the results indicated a low reading. I was advised that because of this my chances of having a Down's Syndrome baby had doubled, and since my age put me in the higher risk group I was looking at some scary statistics.

'The next step was to take an amniocentesis test. I was already experiencing movement of the foetus and was strongly bonded in a way that meant I could never go through with a therapeutic abortion. I spent the few days I had to think about it crying and agonizing, and finally decided to forgo the amnio. My instincts told me that my baby was already what it was going to be, and that I would be able to cope with whatever that was.'

When Rozanne went into labour it seemed to her as though the veil between the living and the dead dissolved. 'I could see and feel all my ancestors, friends and teachers who were on the Other Side. They were standing at the doorway assisting this being into the world of form. This experience was as strong as the experience I had when I went to Mark's grandmother's funeral. It was a moment of undeniable power for me: a revelation of the relationship between life and death. I will never again fear death or birth, because I know that I will not be alone.

'We named our daughter Margaret, which means pearl, and she was that and more. Her full head of hair was dark brown, and her skin had the bronze Native American colouring found way back on my side of the family. A beautiful Indian princess, or perhaps Consuela, my good friend.

'From Margaret I have gained deeper insight into what it means to teach. I have seen that her development is assured – all of the information is packed inside of her and comes out when she is ready. If I don't stand in the way but allow her to experience and express what she needs to do, she will automatically unfold into the little girl and then the woman she already is.

'I think that the inherent knowing of how to be a parent can be found within the heart and mind of every mother and father. I will often know better than any of the experts what my daughter needs. If I can trust my intuition, then learning how to be a parent will automatically unfold. I am finding out more about who I am, because this is the main legacy I will leave my daughter. Not what I have done but being who I am as honestly as I can. This is what I remember about Grandmother Margaret, and this is what my daughter Margaret will remember about me.'

If reincarnation is a possibility, can the child choose the mother he or she wishes to bond with? It may be that Paul chose his present family in Scotland because he knew his mother would be kind to him. When he was about four years old, his mother was washing his face at tea-time when he pulled back suddenly and said: 'Don't wash me there. That's where my mummy hit me.' Her immediate reaction was to say, 'Come on now,' because she was busy and children come out with all kinds of excuses to avoid the ordeal of soap and water. But then she stopped and said: 'Well, tell me about it then.' He said in an abrupt manner, as if she were stupid, 'You know – that's where she hit me and I fell down the stairs and died. Not you, mummy, but the mummy I had before. That's why this time I decided to come to a mummy who would love me.'

But if there is a choice, why would anyone return to a mother with whom they had shared a previous unhappy life? Liz Cornish, a rebirthing expert in London, says: 'The point of existence on Earth is to overcome all problems. When we are reborn we choose the family we are born into because of some unfinished business in our previous existence – to fulfill some need. Why else would we choose what sometimes seem to be such appalling parents? Maybe we have been in different relationships with them in past lives, and this time are trying to get it right.'

Sarah, who also lives in London, sees her problems with her mother as stemming from a past life in which they were also mother and daughter. She has had visions of this past life in which she lived in a slum with a mother who beat her and eventually abandoned her. In these visions 'I see myself standing at the entrance of a long, dark tunnel, protesting that I don't want to go back. I am saying, "I don't want to be born through that woman," meaning my present mother. But I must go down the tunnel. Then I am dragged out into the world before I am ready. Everything around me is hard, cold and white. The light is too bright and hurts my eyes.

'For as long as I can remember I have felt antagonism towards my mother, but my upbringing was normal and I cannot trace it to anything in this life I can remember. I believe it was there already, and that she was the mother who abandoned me before. Perhaps in her soul she wanted to make up for that, but she may have had no choice in that earlier life, and if she was harsh to me then it was because conditions were so hard in the slum.

'There is a parallel here between the psychological theory that people tend to repeat mistakes, placing themselves in similar situations again and again until they discover the root cause of the problems and only then being able to break their behaviour pattern. I am convinced we choose our parents either because there is a bond of love between us and we want to be together again or because of some lesson we have to work out with them.'

In Chapter 4 I mentioned the strong link between Rebecca Parkes and her son Alex, which flourished even though she was a working mother who did not have the time to cultivate the link deliberately, despite her desire to work on it. She believes the link may in fact have started in a previous life. 'About six months before I became pregnant I had this very strong sense of a spirit "hovering",' she told me. 'It wasn't a negative or even impatient feeling – it just gave me a sense of someone nearby waiting to be born. One day I decided to meditate. I wasn't trying to meditate on anything specific, but in my meditation a being came to me and introduced herself. That is, s/he was an androgynous being but seemed to me more female than male.

She told me she had been my daughter in a previous life and was getting ready to be born again. I asked when I'd become pregnant. My husband and I had planned to try in the New Year, and she replied, "January or February – you won't have any problem becoming pregnant." Sure enough I became pregnant the first try, in January.

'I don't know if I imagined all this or what, but the experience was so incredibly real and clear.'

If your child starts talking about a previous life, don't laugh or call in a psychiatrist. Whether he is remembering a past life, some pre-birth memory or saying something about his present bond with you it should be treated with respect. And always remember that if you question him too closely you may get more than you bargained for, as Lilian, a regression expert, found out.

She tried to take her seven-year-old grandson, George, back to a past life to find out if he had had the same mother then. 'Can you see your mum?' she asked him, as he went back into a past life-form. 'Oh yes, she's over there.' 'What's she doing?' 'Swinging from a tree.' Lilian hesitated at this, then asked, 'What's your mum like, George?' 'Furry and brown and cuddly.' 'What are you doing?' 'Oh, messing around, swinging in the branches, scratching a bit and bothering mum.'

With further questioning Lilian confirmed that in this previous life George and his mum had been orang-utans!

8

The Real Magic of Birth

Giving birth is an incredible event. During it you may touch the stars. Alternatively, your husband may *see* stars. During the birth of my third child I shared a ward with a former operating theatre nurse who was unpleasantly surprised that her labour wasn't proceeding like the textbooks said it would. When her husband reminded her she wasn't relaxing according to plan, she clouted him over the head with a bed pan.

You can give birth at home, in the bed in which the child was conceived; or in the back of a taxi on the way to hospital; or on a bean bag surrounded by flowers and crystals, candles and friends; or in an operating theatre amid state-of-the-art technology. It can be the best or worst moment of your life – most likely both. It may go according to plan or be total chaos. How then can you hope to forge a psychic link with your child at this most crucial of moments?

In my opinion we still know far too little about the phenomenon to be able to say with any certainty what should or should not be done. The lightning seems to strike where it will without warning, but there are those who believe that the best thing to do is to put up 'psychic lightning conductors' to try to persuade it to come to earth where they want it to. Waterbirth, for example, is seen by many today as the Holy Grail of maternity. So is it the answer?

Michel Odent is the internationally acclaimed obstetrician who runs a clinic at Pithviers, near Paris. A follower and developer of Leboyer's 'birth without violence' principles (i.e. that the newborn child must be received gently into the world), Odent first used a tank of water as a birthing bed because it eased a mother's labour in many cases. He soon discovered it was also an excellent way of providing a baby with a gentle door into this world.

The researcher Igor Tjarkovsky goes even further into the watertub than Odent, believing that babies born in water are more clairvoyant than those delivered normally and even having a parapsychologist in assistance at the birth[1]. He also believes that the mother and child communicate telepathically during the pre-birth period, and that the newborn infant is open to psychic influences. Tjarkovsky claims that this increased clairvoyance and other paranormal abilities are natural brain functions that can be easily destroyed at birth. 'A gentle transition, both to the world of gravity and to a different way of breathing, opens up completely new possibilities for the human race.'

All this accords with the evidence that gentleness, silence and acceptance are conducive to the mother/child psychic link. But if you really want to know about waterbirths it is best to talk to an expert – i.e., someone who has actually given birth in water. Cindy Bertand-Brozdik of Ontario began working with the technique after the waterbirth of her own son, Jonathan, which she believes helped to foster the psychic link between them. 'We chose to have a waterbirth because it seemed the most gentle and natural way,' she told me. 'But before labour came I had lots of dreams, visions and feelings of the presence of the new person's energy.

'I began dreaming of dolphins. These dreams were so vivid I would wake and smell my hands to see if they smelled of the dolphins I was swimming with and touching. In one dream I was walking along a beach and all along the shoreline were baby dolphins. They had little children's faces and I wondered which one was mine. The last and smallest dolphin/child looked me in the eye, and I knew I was to care for this one. To my amazement

[1] For a fuller account of his work see *Water-Babies* by Eric Sidenbladh, Adam and Charles Black, 1983.

when my son was one-and-a-half years old and sleeping peacefully I looked at his little cherub face and it flashed in my mind that this was the face of that dolphin in my dream.

'At our midwives' advice we told very few people about our plans for a home waterbirth. A few days before my son was born my mother had a dream in which she was picking up a baby out of the water and patting its back so it could breathe. My mother lives across the country, and didn't know what we were planning.'

Cindy's son Jonathan was born at home among friends, and slept that first night between his parents. 'We bought a tub, set it up in our dining-room, filled it with water and waited and waited and waited – emptied the tub, cleaned it again, filled it up and waited some more. My due date came and went: so where was the baby?'

Her husband Rick was not there when the first twinges came. 'A very powerful contraction had me yelling for Rick long-distance on the phone. I heard him say to his colleagues, "Can you hold on? My wife is in labour and I have to go breathe with her." We both laughed through that contraction.'

'Time passed – then it was time to get into the water. It was warm, like my womb temperature. I felt relaxed, safe, secure. My midwife Catherine came in and saw that everything is fine. Our girlfriends arrived, as well as two other midwives, Mary and Jennifer. The energy was beautiful. Rick was behind me holding me while I squatted in the tub. When the contractions got powerful I pulled his hair. He said, "I don't mind, you're doing a great job; I love you." Another contraction – "How many more of these?" I asked, gasping. Catherine said between one and twenty five, but not to be concerned about it, just to go with the flow.

'Four more pushes and out slid a perfect, beautiful, aware, little boy. His eyes were open as he floated calmly in the water. Then he saw us and reached up; we took his face out of the water and held him close while Catherine gave him a little oxygen, because the cord had got a bit flattened. This was by far the most incredible moment of my life. Rick cut the cord, enthralled by its colour.

'We sat around a plate of fruit and shared our feelings: rainbows danced all over the room from crystals hanging in the window. Soft music played, we lit candles, held hands and thanked each other. The evening came and everyone left us. Bedtime came, we placed our newborn son between us and we all drifted off to sleep. New parents were born.

'As our baby grew I could not help sensing a very old soul when looking into his eyes. Although on the outside he seems no different from any other child, he has something special. The few times I would leave him with someone I would jot down the times when I felt messages or thoughts coming into my mind. When I returned home I would find that these were indeed the times when he called out for me. Although Rick does not have feelings and premonitions as I do he is also strongly connected with his son.'

So yes, if you want a waterbirth and it turns out one is possible for you, then it may indeed make it easier for the bonding to flow. But the gentle way is not the only way to the psychic link. Shawna Stewart of Oxford had a hospital birth in which everything went wrong. Nevertheless she believes it was the psychic dialogue which began while her daughter was still in the womb that enabled baby Mela to be born alive and healthy although she was premature. This link also sustained the baby through the difficult weeks she had to spend in special care.

'When I found I was pregnant with my third child I was thrilled. She was very much wanted. But throughout the pregnancy I had a feeling something was wrong. I had the normal blood tests and a scan.

'Everything seemed all right but I couldn't disregard this feeling, so I thought of some of the things that could be wrong with a baby and decided that, no matter what, this was my child and I'd love her. I also felt that whatever happened it would be the right thing, as good and not so good experiences are brought our way because they're what we need for a particular lesson. Anyway, this enabled me to let go of my fear and look forward to the birth of this baby as any other.

'I re-read books I'd enjoyed during my other pregnancies, as well as a book about waterbirth, which was the way I wanted to have my baby. All through pregnancy however I pushed aside the thoughts of "be ready for something different," that tried to push their way in. One night when I was about 22 weeks pregnant I dreamed I'd had the baby in hospital, not at home as I'd planned, but that this little baby born so early was healthy – even talking and sitting up. I woke from the dream feeling strangely relieved. I told my husband about it and said, "But the baby in my dream was a boy, and we're going to have a girl." I thought the relief was a sign that there was nothing wrong, and that that would be the end of the nagging feeling.

'A week and a half later, just as I was going to bed I knew I wanted to order a baby's sheepskin and a tape of womb music. I pulled out the forms and put them in stamped envelopes ready to post in the morning. That night I woke several times to go to the loo, but kept leaking in between. I thought it was strange because I wasn't at all big – still able to wear my jeans, but I was too tired to really think about it so I went back to sleep.

'In the morning I went to town with my husband and two boys. I felt fine at first, but after getting off the bus started leaking a tiny bit. We went for a coffee and when I sat down it dawned on me what was happening. I went straight home, packed a bag, and called the doctor, leaving my husband to follow with the boys. When the doctor arrived I told her I was leaking amniotic fluid and asked what I should do. She advised me to go straight to hospital and have it checked. I was right.

'I spent the next four days in hospital, very anxious to go home and rest in my own bed with my children near me but also strangely confident and strong. I never doubted the baby would live even though the medical profession seemed to feel it their duty to disillusion me. I felt that my tiny baby was reassuring me, giving me strength. I was terribly worried about the psychological effect being physically harassed and separated from me would have on my baby if she were premature; but I had an inner calm voice that made me feel it was all right. I knew this little girl. She was courageous and sweet. She didn't need a frightened mother. When after four days in hospital I went into labour I knew my mental communication with my daughter was going to hold us both together.

'Through twelve hours of the strongest pains I've ever experienced I kept a communication going with her. I let her know I was all right and could cope and that she'd be fine. I was left alone in a large dark room with a bowl to throw up in and one to use as a loo. The nurse, who couldn't examine me because of the risk of infection, had sent my husband away, told me I probably had an irritable uterus, and said I should go to sleep and it would probably all stop! I kindly told her that much as I'd like to agree, I'd been in labour before and just wanted her to make sure things were ready in case this 24-week-old baby did arrive soon. She said it wouldn't have much chance anyway, and to think about my own health! I calmed myself and mentally found a quiet place in my mind to rest with my daughter. I experienced the contractions with her, from her perspective. It was unbelievable! I felt the way a squeezing contraction enabled my heart to pump the blood all around my body warm and fast, and felt the surging adrenalin. Mela and I were together in the womb. Then I was in the uterus massaging her. Then we were one – until I hit transition.

'I felt desperate panic for the first time, lost communication with Mela for a moment while I rang for the nurse and told her I couldn't take this any more because this baby was coming now! She didn't believe me because I'd looked asleep to her while I was in my inner communication with my daughter. She consented to examine me – then *she* was the one panicking and I was fine – even happy.

'They hadn't got anything ready – so after dashing down the corridors with me to the delivery room they had literally to hold Mela back while a ventilator was hooked up. The nurse gave me words of encouragement and apologized for sending my husband away. But I felt relieved, strong and confident that all would be well. Once they were ready I delivered Mela. I was shocked by her tiny size and beauty. She was like a doll, only 1 lb 4 oz and bright pink, much pinker than my other two babies had been. They whisked her over to the incubator before I could even touch her. That's the only part I regret.

'During the following months while Mela was in special care we shared hours of mental communication. It was painful being away from her, so I spent nearly all of my waking hours by her side. I sang to her, talked to her and stroked her, but we thought together for much more of the time each day. Many times I'd come in to be told they'd given her a slight sedative or that she'd had lots of bradycardias, but while I was with her she didn't play up. Although her progress was slow it was steady, with no major complications.

'When she was born her eyes were still sealed. The first time I held her was the first time she opened them. She stared straight at me; I could hardly believe it was real.

'Mela is now a very healthy little girl. She'll be four soon. She's happy, kind-hearted, thoughtful and wise beyond her years. She comforts and loves her big brothers when they're upset, and takes endless delight in her little sister Arwen, who was born at home in a birthing pool 29th November 1990. I'm still learning from Mela, and wonder if she'll ever remember any of what we went through. I've learned it's the soul of the person we should all communicate with – the body holds comparatively little relevance.'

Shawna's link with her child at birth was a very spiritual one, though the circumstances were far from ideal. In Chapter Two we met Ingrid Millar, who diagnosed by psychic means her baby son Rory's life-threatening illness. She was closely bonded with

Rory. His birth, like Mela's, was anything but a magical, gentle process, but Ingrid found that the bond with him was stronger than that with her second son, with whom her labour was easier and to whom, on the surface, she was closer.

'I was thirty-six hours in labour with Rory, and he had to be delivered by forceps. The cord was tightly wrapped twice round his neck, so I was very lucky to have him at all, let alone for him to be perfect. He just didn't want to come out. The minute he was born (at 6 a.m.) the light streamed in and I was there, after all the pain, holding the most beautiful child I had ever seen. I just couldn't take my eyes away from him. He looked like a cherub, though in spite of his "butter wouldn't melt in his mouth" looks, he can be a little devil.

'After Rory was born I just couldn't leave him alone. It was my first big love affair. They wouldn't let him sleep in my room so I used to hobble to the nursery to gaze at him. I always went straight to his cot, though there were eight or nine other babies. I could not believe it would ever be possible to feel anything so special again.'

Leo's birth was by contrast slapstick comedy, but nevertheless was tinged with a magic that 'experts' claim could only come from a quiet, spiritually-directed birth. This time Ingrid touched the stars in the down-to-earth surroundings of the hospital's laundry cupboard. 'With Leo I delayed going into hospital for as long as possible because labour had been so painful with Rory. By the time I finally got to hospital they'd given up on me and given my birth room to someone else. So the only place for me to have the baby was in the laundry supply room. My bed was squeezed in between the towels and rubber gloves. My husband Kevin settled me in and then dashed off to pick up Rory from the childminder.

'Suddenly it was as if I was no longer in control. My body took over completely, a physical wave from the top of my head to the tip of my toes, the most ultimate world-shattering, orgasmic feeling. I was deliriously happy. It was the best experience in my whole life, but I had nothing to do with it. I had no will or mind, I just knew the baby was coming. The nurse opened the window and screamed at the top of her voice for Kevin to come back.

'Kevin was at the front gates of the hospital, but he hailed a passing laundry van which drove back at top speed to the entrance and Kevin arrived just as Leo came out in the most incredible whoosh. Leo is my soul-mate. He is so like me, physically and in every other way. I dote on him and am tremendously tolerant with him. I relate to him.

'In spite of this it is with my first son Rory that I have this incredible intuitive bond, though he sometimes drives me mad. I have always felt that he needed me to look after him. He has always been sensitive and highly strung. I always woke before Rory woke, but I didn't with Leo. I knew Leo was all right. It was more than exhaustion that let me sleep till Leo yelled.

'I breast-fed Rory until six weeks before Leo was born, and I felt no one could have given a child more.'

Ingrid's experiences show us again how fruitless it is to try to predict, let alone influence, a mother's instincts. By all accounts it should have been Leo with whom she had a psychic bond – the product of an easy happy birth, a happy-natured child whose character was akin to her own. But Ingrid sees the psychic bond as rooted in the need of the child rather than what the parent would wish for.

Of course, every mother would wish for a gentler birth and good early postnatal experiences. But the deeper psychic bonding, as indeed any form of mother/child link, isn't a one-off. If the birth goes wrong there is the rest of the child's life to get it right.

At the private Garden Hospital in London a mother is encouraged to consider all aspects of pregnancy, spiritual as well as physical. Mothers-to-be take classes in yoga and hear lectures on the psychical aspects of birth. Nevertheless, Yehudi Gordon, an obstetrician there, believes that flexibility is essential, for the best birth plans can go wrong when Mother Nature refuses to co-operate. The most ardent natural birther may need anaesthetic, feeling a failure as a result. He believes that the new methods are in danger of becoming as inflexible as the old-fashioned ones. He has been quoted as saying that a rigid birth plan, complete with friends, pillows, candles and pictures, can be just as dangerous as the old way of doing everything according to hospital protocol. 'It is important,' he has said, 'to be able to go with the flow, without feeling a failure, even if a Caesarean is necessary.'

During the birth a mother might share with her infant glimpses of another dimension. For at no other time, except at the point of death, do people move so far from the earthly plane. Again it is not predictable, so you cannot plan for it by developing your spirituality in a conscious way. Often it is through the more painful, difficult births that the psychic world reveals itself, and while you may not be lucky enough to experience the uplifting sensations of a gentle birth, nevertheless the separating of your and your infant's psyches can cause some pretty amazing spiritual fireworks. Many women have told me that although they had received no drugs they saw dead relatives, often female ones, who 'popped into the labour room to keep an eye on things'.

When Britt Courtney of Boca Raton in Florida gave birth to her second child, Amanda, she felt that her relatives who had died gathered close to celebrate the new life. 'Amanda's birth was a lovely, happy event, with no drugs. My two sisters were my labour partners because my husband had flu. My daughter was born at 1 p.m., and that evening and throughout the night my room was a spiritual gathering place – a celebration party for the birth of Amanda Patricia. They all seemed to have come to share our joy.

'My late father visited, and I sensed his loving, happy laughter and felt his happiness for my happiness. My deceased grandfather Jacob and grandmother Amanda came together to visit, too, as did my uncle and aunt and my deceased older brother Johnnie, who gave me his "older brother proud smile". There may have been more, but the one there longest was Amanda's grandmother, my husband's mother, Pat. She was just so happy.

'I am a registered nurse and childbirth educator, very practical and slightly cynical. I've always thought of myself as a spiritual person but never zealous or fanatic about anything. I don't look for psychic or spiritual experiences. They just happen. The times I've awakened before the kids are endless, as are the times I've arrived at the scene of a potential accident in time to prevent it (although I'm still a cautious mom).

'Near Christmas time, when my son was one-and-a-half, I was in our living room alone with him and I felt his grandmother Patricia come into the room and visit her grandson. She let me know how happy her grandson made her and how much she loves him (I could sense her being there and her feelings). Since then I have sensed her presence two other times.'

Grandmother Pat may well have been in at the birth of Britt's son as well, but Britt has no way of knowing because the child was delivered by Caesarean while she was under general anaesthetic.

Lizzie Parker's dead aunt was not content to sit and watch during the birth of her niece, especially because the doctors appeared to be getting things wrong. Lizzie, who lives in Reading, Berkshire, was having her third child, and would have liked her mum's help to sort the doctor out. But mother was looking after Lizzie's other two children.

The doctor wanted to put a drip in Lizzie's arm, as he said labour would go on for a long time and she needed something to speed things up. Lizzie didn't want the drip in as she was sure that she would give birth any minute, but she was too weak to argue. Lizzie suddenly became aware of her favourite aunt Eileen, who had died two months before, standing by the bedside. Every time the doctor tried to put in the drip Eileen took it out. The doctor couldn't understand why the drip kept falling out, but he didn't have time to get to the bottom of the mystery because five minutes later baby Heather was born.

Sometimes a labouring woman can call on the angels to help her. In the case of Carol Newfeld, an editor from Santa Fe, New Mexico, it was the Archangel Michael she called upon at the birth of her daughter. 'I always had a great sense of joy and communion with my baby in utero,' she said. 'At the time of her birth (five years ago) I entered labour peacefully and experienced a gentle, stress-free and harmonious first stage. In fact I was 10 centimetres dilated when my husband called the midwife. I should add that I felt a strong spiritual bond with my midwife from the moment we met, and knew that her skill and intuition and our bond would be a very vital part of the birth. Then suddenly my second-stage labour appeared to stop. My daughter was evidently posterior (lying on her back, head down), and was not in distress at all, so we all felt good about allowing the labour to take as long as it needed. After three hours of pushing, however, I was exhausted, and a sense of fear and hopelessness was affecting each of us – my midwife was particularly tired, since she had been up the previous night birthing my friend's baby. Then there was a clear moment for me between contractions.

'I stood up on the bed. I felt strength enter me and I asked for help from the Archangel Michael – a being whom I've experienced throughout my life as a guide and protector – androgynous, though carrying a male focus. A clarity of purpose became apparent: each person knew exactly what he or she should do: the fear dissipated, the anxiety went and the lucidity for right action and decision-making was present. I pushed my baby far enough down for my midwife, with the help of another person, to turn her – a painful but incredible manoeuvre which required absolute attunement between me and the two of them. My daughter was born within minutes of this action. She is named Mikhaila, as she clearly has a resonance with Archangel Michael. Even three weeks after her birth friends would comment on the quality in our house – one person said it felt like an ashram. In a more general sense I was aware of birth angels present – but the "sword of Michael" was what was most needed.

'We have a little ritual at bedtime: my daughter puts her hand on her heart – that is her way of contacting her guardian angel.'

In the course of my research I have come across a strange phenomenon, which I have called the near-birth experience (NBE), in which a woman during labour has an experience akin to what we know of near-death experiences. She may rise out of her body and see visions of beautiful places, or converse with shining forms. Why this happens we don't know, except that perhaps when a new life comes forth and the mother and infant's psyches begin to form a separate existence, something pretty special happens. These experiences perhaps more than any other suggest that the bond between mother and child is not rooted in the physical nor entirely in the psychological but in the magical realms we last accepted as a child.

Karen had a traumatic labour, though her own life was not in danger. However, it soon became obvious that everything was not going as it should and that the baby was in great difficulty. 'I was turned on to my front with a gas-and-air mask over my face. As I lay in this position I can remember saying "Please, help me, God," and then I felt myself rising out of my body. I found myself in a dark place (almost like being in space). My mother's face then came towards me out of the dark and said, "You can't stay here. You have to move on." I said "To where?" There was no answer, and then her face left and my father's face appeared and said the same thing, and then my husband's face and the same words. It was so real. I then felt I had to get back into my body, and said or thought, "I'm not ready for this yet. I want to go back." As I started to draw down to my body I had a flash – almost like a picture of the world. I opened my eyes and said to the nurse, "I have just died." They laughed at me. "You just fainted," they said. I then said to myself, "Well, I wouldn't have believed it either if it hadn't happened to me."

'The point I can't understand is that my husband and mother

and father are still alive, and yet they were there. I'd just like to add that my baby was born safely, and is now healthy two-year-old boy.'

Karen's experience was remarkably similar to a child's near-death experience. Studies made of the subject report that children tend to see living rather than dead relatives. Could it be Karen was sharing the experience with her child, and so viewed it through a child's eyes? The nurses laughed. Sometimes it is difficult for professionals to cope with the unusual, for their competence depends on their being 'in control'. Only if they possess great sensitivity and confidence in themselves as people behind the mask of professionalism can they relate to these kinds of phenomena at all. Physical or psychic, it was a very significant moment for Karen.

It is perhaps easier for some to accept Karen's experience was the effect of the gas and air. A magic bond forged in birth is something many adults find it uncomfortable to accept, particularly those who like to believe they have absolutely no connection with their own mother.

Doctors Andrew and Penny Stanway point out in *Choices in Childbirth* (Pan, 1984) that 'Birth being the astonishing and wonderful process it is – it is hardly surprising that it is sometimes associated with the supernatural. Some even interpret the otherworldliness of labour with women as "hanging between life and death". '

But whatever doctors say, at the end of the day what is important is a woman's belief in the experience. After all, they are the ones who actually went through it.

Even when the woman's life is in danger, what separates a near-birth experience from a near-death experience is that it is the bond with the baby that calls the mother back to the everyday world.

The story of Pauline's own birth during the Second World War was told to her many times by her mother. 'My mother suffered a very prolonged and complicated delivery at home, supervised by a young and very inexperienced midwife. As a result my mother was in a state of shock and her heart was failing by the time the family doctor had arrived. The doctor was trying to resuscitate her with the now old-fashioned technique of heart massage when my mother went into cardiac arrest. At that point my mother said she felt only a wonderful sense of relaxation and total freedom from pain. She felt as if she were floating through a pale blue mist, smelling the perfume of innumerable flowers, hearing music and singing sweeter than anything she had ever heard in this world. She felt the presence of warm and friendly people, and was convinced that soon she would emerge from the mist and be able to identify these unseen presences. At that moment she heard a baby cry and a voice saying, "You have a baby now – you must take care of it." She decided to return to her body, and found herself back in the world.'

Pauline's mother often said her greatest fear was that she might be unable to return to that wonderful place she had visited.

For Alison it was also the bond with her first child that gave her the desire to return. She recalled: 'Everything happened very quickly. I left home at ten past five in the morning and my second son was born at ten to six, and that's when it happened. I haemorrhaged just after the birth, and all I remember was the two midwives present saying, "Quick, get a doctor." I never had any gas and air or injection, and by the time they got the doctor I remember them slapping my face and saying, "Don't go to sleep."

'After a few minutes I felt myself rising away from my body floating above myself, and I came to a place where I saw streams and beautiful gardens and I wanted to carry on. I also saw my whole self lying on the bed. I could see my whole body below although I floated upwards, and suddenly I thought of my oldest son, who was only two. I gripped the sides of the bed and pulled myself down. The experience gave me a terrific fright.'

Alison said that although this incident happened nine years ago she still remembers its terror; however, she also remembers its pleasure, and says: 'If that's death then I reckon nobody need be afraid of it.'

For some women such an experience is not seen as entirely positive. It can strip away all they thought they knew, and if they cannot incorporate a religious or spiritual significance to it, they can find the whole process very unnerving. But then the mother-baby bond can be a very unnerving though exciting thing. Once you have a child, nothing is the same again.

Dr Peter Fenwick is Consultant Neuropsychiatrist at the Maudsley Hospital in London. He is also President of IANDS UK (International Association for Near-Death Studies). When I asked him about women's near-birth experiences, he said: 'I believe [that] your idea that near-birth experiences could possibly be related to the bonding process – a viewpoint I have not heard discussed before – raises interesting implications. I would suggest that one argument against it would be that as near-birth experiences are extremely rare it will only make a small difference to the bonding process and thus is unlikely to have a survival value. However I think we need more data before we can come to that viewpoint.

'From the point of view of physiology, near-birth experiences are very similar to near-death experiences, and these are thought to be a disorder of brain function. There are really severe difficulties attributing subjective experience totally to brain function as we, as yet, have no scientific models of this.'

In a paper written by Dr Fenwick and David Lorimer, the chairman of IANDS, for the *New Scientist* (5 August, 1989), they point out: 'We know that we live in a world where love, beauty, meaning and value are part of our daily lives, indeed are the most important aspects of our world. This subjective experience is what we call consciousness, and even if the physicists have no place for it, it has still to be reckoned with.'

Until the relevant theoretical models are devised, mothers will go on having these experiences and finding out that the bond of motherhood is indeed a powerful one.

I said at the beginning of this chapter that giving birth is an incredible event. But what if it is a disaster from start to finish? You may need drugs because your labour is one agonizing contraction from the beginning, and then after hours of labour still end up having to have a Caesarean Section. Afterwards you find the baby you wanted to breast-feed from the word go has been given a bottle – not that you could breast-feed right then anyway because your middle feels as though it has been kicked by a mule. Then you find you've one of those non-textbook babies who wants feeding every half hour day and night and bawls between the feeds with colic. Don't panic, it's unlikely you'll be afflicted with all these hassles (your name's not Mrs Job, is it?). You can't say, 'I've changed my mind – please put the baby back,' though at the time that might seem the most logical course. But at the worst, many women have told me that they still bonded in every way with their baby even when everything went wrong. Tomorrow really is another day, with more time to discover these psychic bonds, however unlikely that may seem as you sit on your cushion nursing your stitches. You have the rest of your life to get it right, as did Rachel Hey, whom we met in Chapter 3.

Rachel says: 'When Jacob was first born I didn't feel love for him. I only felt an incredibly strong need to protect him. I had a very long labour – 24 hours from the onset of painful contractions – and by the end of this I was absolutely exhausted. I eventually had an epidural, so when Jacob was finally born we were both too tired to get to know each other. I had wanted to breast-feed him as soon as he was born, but he was full of mucus and was finding breathing difficult. His first feed was from a bottle because he was kept in special care for observation overnight.

'I had expected to love him immediately but I didn't. All I had was this overwhelming need to protect him. I would be brought to tears at the thought of anything ever hurting him. Two days after the birth I can remember watching him sleep and suddenly being hit by love for him. I was very relieved by this because I had been very worried I might never love him.'

Louise Richardson, of Mississauga, Ontario, believes that a traumatic birth can adversely affect both mother and baby for some time afterwards. Although psychologists from Freud onwards have presented a very negative picture of the irreversibility of early psychological damage, Louise is convinced that by using the psychic link she was able to reassure her daughter and so give her a positive outlook on life.

'When I was in labour with my daughter,' said Louise, 'the nurses in hospital were particularly brutal. At one point during labour one of them was so rough I had a strange feeling my daughter felt it, although she didn't jump or anything. After she was born I only held her for about a minute, and didn't see her again until four hours later. I can only hope the nurses were more gentle with her than they were with me! It turned out the nurses were in the midst of some rather bitter contract negotiations at the time.

'After my daughter was born she was very jittery for the first six months. She would jump at even the faintest sound, and she never just closed her eyes and went to sleep when she was tired. She always cried herself to sleep in my arms. She would also cry inconsolably whenever anyone else held her or when I put her in a baby chair or swing. I always had the suspicion this was because of the brutality I endured when she was born. After about six months of this behaviour it became almost unbearable for both my daughter and myself. One night in the rocking chair I had a mental conversation with her, but this time it was deliberate. I reassured her that I would always be with her, I'd never let anyone do anything hurtful to her, and that what had happened in the hospital would never happen again, so how about calling a truce?

'The next night she started sleeping through, and was generally a lot more calm. At first I thought it was my imagination or wishful thinking, but my husband, the neighbours and my parents all commented on the change in her behaviour. I hadn't told my parents or the neighbours about what I'd "said" to the baby.'

So what can we deduce from all these angels, dead relatives, watertubs and laundry cupboards? Be prepared for anything, and give birth the way which suits you if you can. It's not an endurance test but a means to the very best end of all – your baby. And be prepared to find out everything you can. Make two birth plans: the worst and the best. The first time I was pregnant I refused to go to the antenatal class on Caesarean section because I knew I was going to give birth naturally. I did need an emergency Caesarean, and because I knew nothing about them it was a terrible shock. In contrast, when I needed a Caesarean with my fifth child I was wide awake holding the baby while the doctors reassembled my insides, and it was one of the best experiences of my life.

Even if the last thing you want after giving birth is the baby, you haven't ruined it for life whatever researchers tell you about the first sixteen hours affecting the child's chances of getting a Ph.D. You have the rest of your life to put it right. Relax and talk things over with your infant – after all you are a psychic team. Ultimately in any birth it is the well-being of you and the infant that is paramount. Twenty years on your six-footer won't really hold it against you that you overdosed on the gas and air. What he will remember are all the magical moments – built on love, not guilt – that have grown up between you.

I leave the chapter with the words of Maria Cadaxa, our midwife friend from Tucson, Arizona: 'I have definitely seen golden light surround the emerging baby on several occasions. I have not established a pattern of who this happens to or why, except that these children are coming to loving, prepared parents. Born in the light of love? It is quite an awesome happening to see this light and perceive the beauty and sacredness of birth. It is like seeing through the door into another world.'

Happy Birth Day.

9

The Growing Connection

You have the rest of your life to get it right, as I said in the last chapter, and for many mothers this has been a comforting thought while whirling round like a dervish, unable to believe one 8-lb bundle could cause so much work. Children do grow up, and sometimes the psychic bond grows with them – but not in the way you might expect.

Take heart: your huge, strangely dressed teenager that stomps around the house will no longer be picking up your thoughts on a regular basis. He will be too busy broadcasting his own very loudly. And that once sweet little girl who now sulks for weeks on end – usually in the bathroom – will be far too busy trying to keep her own thoughts secret to eavesdrop on yours. That stage of psychic communication comes back when teenagers become human beings and harmony is restored on the earthly as well as the psychic plane.

The adolescent declares he would rather die than follow mum's advice. But since your beloved baby bird has now found really heart-stopping hobbies, many of which involve wheels and powerful engines, the protective bond often has to work overtime.

Elise from Dallas, Texas, believes that a psychic sign made her nag her son into taking the advice which saved his life. 'My youngest son bought a motor cycle when he was 18. He lived about 25 miles from us and came by our house every afternoon when he got off work, and stayed between 15 minutes and half an hour. I'd fuss at him for not wearing his crash helmet, yet every day he came by without it again. There seemed no point in arguing with him. This one afternoon I was sitting at the dinner table looking outside and talking to my husband when my son drove up. When he walked in it was as if he was covered in a light, a glowing blue light all over. The thought came to me as clear as anything I ever had come to mind that the light all over my son was death. I knew it as well as anything I ever knew, a clear, positive feeling. I looked at David and said, "Son, why can't you wear your helmet? You are going to die if you don't wear it."

'Boys hate their mothers to try to make them do anything. They feel they are old enough to decide for themselves. My son did, too. But I knew I had to make him wear it this day or he would die. He got uptight for a minute and then yelled, "All right, all right, if it will get you off my back, I'll wear my helmet." He'd left one at our house, so he left with it on.

'Twenty minutes later and some miles on, a 16-year-old girl in a car turned left straight in front of my son. He had no time to do anything but hit the car. He was slammed into the windscreen and cut his arm and shoulder really badly, going up and over the car onto the tarmac several yards behind her. His helmet had a crack four inches long in the back of it. He was carried to the hospital in bad shape and was in intensive care for three days with internal injuries. I never saw that light around him after that, but I know he would have died that day without his helmet. I've always been able to see the danger to my children before it happened, and have, to my way of thinking, been able to counter it before it came to pass. I can't see these things where I'm concerned, though.'

The hostilities engendered by adolescence don't then seem to affect the underlying bond, they just reserve it for crises, especially those when the self-assured teenager suddenly feels five again and wants mum to put the world right. Of course it's most likely the adolescent won't ask for help, but he or she still expects to get it. "Am I supposed to be a mind-reader?" you snap back at some smart comment from your know-all 15-year-old. The rebirthing expert Liz Cornish believes that rebellion on the part of the teenager is an important part of giving him the impetus to flee the nest, and so is healthy as well as inevitable.

Sometimes a mother's instinct is a vital tool in overcoming the teenager's reluctance to admit all isn't right beneath the cool exterior. Belinda, who lives in the south of England, had not always seen eye-to-eye with her 17-year-old daughter Judy. So it was with a certain amount of relief that she went off for a few days holiday with her husband, brother and sister-in-law in the West Country, leaving Judy with a full freezer, enough money, and instructions to go to her grandmother round the corner if there were any problems. Judy enjoyed her freedom and the run of the house on the occasions mum and dad went off. Belinda had been on holiday four days when, as she told me: 'I had a sudden feeling that something dreadful was wrong with my daughter, not the normal teenage escapades, and that I must go home at once. I went to my husband and said "I'm sorry but we've got to go home right away. Something's terribly wrong with Judy." My husband said I was being stupid, especially as I couldn't tell him anything definite, only that she needed me. I tried to explain to my sister-in-law because I knew I was spoiling everyone's holiday. But I insisted that if my husband wouldn't drive me I'd go back on the train. All the way home my husband said I was being an absolute fool and an over-anxious mother.

'When we got home, Judy was in a terrible state. She hadn't told me before we went away but she was pregnant, and in those four days had suffered a miscarriage. She had phoned her gran for help, but Gran could be very narrow-minded and just didn't want to know. My daughter didn't know whom to turn to. She'd even been too frightened to call a doctor.

'Though Judy and I had had our rows (and still do), and hadn't even been especially close in a conventional way, Judy was so relieved to see me. We were able to sort things out. It turned out she had been pregnant with twins and had lost one of them. We talked it through and I promised to help her to look after the second child when it was born. In a funny way we started to look forward to it. But she miscarried the other twin, too. Had I not gone back who knows what would have happened? I was there when she needed me.'

Teenagers and vehicles more powerful than a push-bike are not a happy marriage, as we saw with Elise's son and the motor-bike crash. Though there were no major adolescent conflicts between Daphne Plowman and her sons, nevertheless she experienced two psychic 'wheelies' concerning them. When her second son, Alistair, turned the car over in a ditch in thick snow it wasn't the RAC he called out but 'Help, Mum.' Alistair was out driving in March 1982 when an unexpected blizzard hit Scotland. 'I was standing by the dining-room window of our house in Glasgow watching enormous snowflakes landing on the back garden,' said Daphne. 'when I suddenly heard Alistair's voice calling "Mum, help me." I got very agitated and said to John, my husband, "There's something wrong with Ali." John said it was just the snow making me nervous, but it never had before.

'About an hour later Ali appeared at the back door in a terrible state, covered in snow. "I've rolled the car but I've got it home," he said. Apparently the car had skidded off the main road about two miles from the house and gone through a hedge and down a bank into a field. Alistair, all by himself, had managed to right the heavy car and get it back onto the road and drive it home.

'When we saw where he had gone through the hedge and where he had landed with the car we could hardly believe he could have managed it. Had I managed to send him the extra strength he needed so badly? I asked him later what he was thinking at the time. He replied: "I think I said 'Mum, help' or something like that." '

Her second 'other channel contact' concerned her third son, Mike, and was more of a psychic early warning.

'Early in August 1984 we were on holiday in Sussex with our caravan when I had a horrible dream. My third son, Mike, came into our lounge/dining-room and stood near the desk. Blood was streaming from his forehead and he said, "Mum, I've smashed Dad's car." '

Despite the dream, the holiday passed off without incident. At the end of the month Daphne and her husband John were back home in Scotland and John, who is a teacher, was due to go up to the school's Outdoor Centre at Glen Etive with a party of schoolboys. 'I was to take John's car and the food and two boys who were inclined to be car sick,' said Daphne. 'It is a very winding journey up the side of Loch Lomond and over Rannoch Moor. My husband was driving the school mini-bus with the rest of the party. The day before the expedition my mother was taken ill at her home in East Lothian. I had to cancel my trip and another staff wife took my place. Instead I drove to Mum in John's car. She had recovered sufficiently by the Saturday for me to drive home again to Glasgow. I planned to join John's expedition on the Sunday, but John told me to have a day's rest and come up on the Monday. He rang me at lunchtime on Sunday, and while we were speaking Mike came into the room and asked to borrow the car to go with his friends to Loch Lomond. Three hours later, the scene of my dream re-enacted itself. Mike had had a burst tyre in the car and it had slammed into a stone dyke. His forehead was cut and blood streamed from it. All the other occupants of the car were unharmed. The car was a write off. Mike's words were, "Mum, I've smashed Dad's car." He had.

'The change of plans due to Mum's illness meant that the car was available for Mike when it should have been 90 miles away.'

So we are back to the question that came up in Chapter 2 on premonitions concerning our children. What is the point in knowing what's going to happen if you can't prevent it? Daphne's son Ali may well have benefited from the fact that Daphne was able, even without realizing it, to send him strength while he was in trouble, but with Mike she could hardly have confined him to a push-bike on the strength of a dream. But at least she was somewhat prepared, so that when her son arrived, shocked and hurt, she could concentrate not on her own feelings but on caring and comforting him.

It is not only motorized hazards that threaten our offspring in the urban jungle, but also the minefields of human relationships. Grown-up children can make mistakes, especially when choosing partners. Often a mother can only stand by and watch, ready to pick up the pieces if it all goes wrong. Few relationships will end as traumatically as that of Lucille Hurd's daughter, Donitza, but if they should it is comforting to think that mother might be keeping an eye on you even when she is thousands of miles away. Lucille was in Britain and her daughter in the US, when one night she had a terrifying dream. 'It concerned my daughter, who unfortunately had fallen for a man who swaggered around like Errol Flynn. He nearly killed my young and beautiful daughter in her Manhattan apartment. She cried out to me the moment he attacked her with a knife. I woke up thunderstruck and perspiring, and sent out loving and protective thoughts to her. Miraculously she survived, I believe because I was with her then, as I had been with her throughout her childhood when she called out for me.'

Fortunately most flights from the maternal nest are happier ones, though they may cause a few sleepless nights for mum. From the moment kids learn to undo the straps of their buggy, you can't stop them wandering. With the advancing years comes the tendency to make these steps big ones, and your erstwhile babe can end up in all kinds of exotic (and danger-ridden) places. Why is it kids never choose the safe seaside ten miles down the road to go and find their destiny? Of course they promise to phone, but . . .So what do you do after worrying and fretting at the silence from Katmandu? It depends: if you are lucky enough to have a psychic mobile phone link, as Doris from Manchester did, then you do as she did.

Doris told me that in 1981 her daughter Susan went with her friend to Corsica for a month. 'She wrote and phoned a few times, and promised to phone on June 9, my husband's birthday. June 9 came with no call from Susan. As each day went by without a call from her our anxiety grew. We asked the police if they could help contact her, but they said that as she was over 18 there was nothing they could do at that stage. By the 19th we were really upset. My husband appealed to me, asking if I had any idea what could have happened to Susan (as I seemed to have a mental link to Susan he thought perhaps I would know). At that moment I had no idea. He went out for a walk, leaving me with my thoughts. I began to think about my own mother, who had died six months previously. She had been fond of Susan, and I found myself talking to her in my head, asking her to look after Susan. The answer came immediately; without a doubt I "knew" what had happened. It was as though a great weight had been lifted from me. When my husband came back I told him with complete conviction that he could stop worrying; Susan was all right. The reason she hadn't phoned was that on the ninth, my husband's birthday, she couldn't find a phone. And on the subsequent days there hadn't been anything particular to report to us, so she hadn't bothered to call. Within the hour the phone rang. It was Susan, and she said almost word for word what I had told my husband.'

Jane picked up the distress signals of her almost full-grown fledgling on the other side of the world and was set to go and find him when news came that he was safe though definitely distressed. She woke in the middle of the night feeling very ill and frightened, and felt sure something was happening to her son. He was in India at the time, location unknown. She begged her husband to raise the fare so she could go and find him. Shortly after this her son wired home for the return fare. His friends had travelled on to Katmandu, leaving him camping alone. He had been delirious for three days with what eventually turned out to be hepatitis.

In Chapter 4 about toddlers sending distress signals, Louise recalled that when her small son was lost she wasn't afraid because she knew he was all right and was still with her. Why then can't this communication be used regularly and systematically to locate missing children and young adults? In the case of missing teenagers, perhaps some don't want to be found and switch off. And in tragic cases, perhaps the fear of mother and child is so great that the reflex won't work.

Doreen Muir of Wiltshire was able to use the psychic link with her daughter to break through the barriers of military secrecy. Her daughter had just joined the army, and regularly wrote home cheerful letters that maintained that everything was going very well. But Doreen began to feel certain that something was wrong, and after a particularly vivid dream in which her daughter was very distressed she trusted her instinct that this was more than a maternal free-floating anxiety, it was a cry for help from her soldier girl. She confronted her daughter, who admitted that she had got herself into serious financial difficulty, and Doreen was then able to help her sort things out.

Doreen also enjoyed a harmonious relationship with her son Eric, who was still living at home, and their everyday link had carried on from his childhood. Indeed, Eric found as he spread his wings that he could put the psychic link to good use. Doreen says: 'When he was in his late teens Eric had a habit of forgetting his key, and would quietly wait outside using telepathy to wake me. Sometimes it would be well after midnight when I woke up and realized he was there. He was a bit embarrassed to tell me how he had woken me up. He says he "thought" to me, calling me in his mind, and after a while I woke realizing he needed me to open the front door.'

Peggy Rouse, also of Wiltshire, had a very bad relationship with her own mother. She had rejected Peggy from an early age, and this perhaps is why Peggy has fostered warm, close links with her own children that have continued right through their adolescence and adulthood. In these relationships telepathic communication is so routine that, as Peggy told me, it is only when the other party replies out loud to an unspoken conversation that it becomes surprising. Peggy believed right from the start that it was important to treat her own and indeed all children as individuals with rights, and her telepathic abilities continue to work with her grandchildren.

Peggy recalled for me just three of the numerous incidents spanning her children's adolescent and grown-up years. 'When my daughter Penny was 16 we were about to go shopping when she said: "I could do with one, too." "What do you mean?" I asked. "A Guinness when we've finished the shopping." Then she stopped: "Wasn't that what you said?"

'Well of course I hadn't said anything out loud, but that was exactly what I'd been thinking.

'My son and I used to drive the same car. He and I were used to saying the same thing and thinking the same thing. We were living in New Zealand at the time, and because he was only 15 I only allowed him to drive in the countryside. One day as we were driving along the thought came into my mind: "Oh I hope we don't run into a police trap along here." My son pulled the car over and I slid into the driver's seat. Then I realized and said: "Why did we do that?" because it wasn't a normal place for a police trap and I certainly hadn't said anything out loud. "I thought there might be a police trap," he said.

'When my children were all grown up we arranged to pay a mortgage on a smallholding between us as an investment. One Sunday afternoon I said to my daughter Jo, who was living with me, "Isn't the mortgage on the property due tomorrow? I hope Penny doesn't forget to pay, I'd better ring her." So I rang straight away. Penny answered and before I could say anything, told me, "I got it out of the cupboard five minutes ago. It's the 23rd tomorrow, isn't it?" '

All these instances could be put down to familiarity: for example, as the mortgage was due Penny would have been thinking about it anyway, and perhaps expecting her mum to be worried she'd forget. But it's the timing that makes these cases so remarkable. Penny just continued her mother's unspoken communication, without a break.

Routine telepathic contact is very much a by-product of a close, accepting family, and persists even when the children are grown up. The advantage is that even when family members are far apart they can continue to provide one another support. One interesting factor is that this telepathy occurs where there is sufficient freedom and independence physically and emotionally for such communication to flow free. The psychic bond is not made of chains; it is a safety line between you and your children as each climbs his own mountains. There is no need to fear that by allowing such bonds to continue you are smothering your children. It is the women who are anxious to manipulate and keep their growing children near them as an antidote to loneliness whose anxieties and resentments block the channel automatically.

Many grown-up women can recall picking up the phone to call mum and finding it is engaged because mum was trying to phone them. This communication is very much a two-way thing. A woman may be fuming over an injustice but not want to bother anyone with her problems, or may just be feeling alone or off-colour. The phone rings, and it is her grown-up daughter from the other end of the country asking, 'What's up, Mum?'

Jean, who lives in the south of England, has three grown-up children. She and her daughters always know when something is wrong with one another, even though they are spread throughout Britain. One night Jean woke at about three o'clock convinced something was wrong with her youngest daughter, Sally, who is in her 20s. Jean didn't feel she could ring in the middle of the night in case it was a false alarm, so instead she tossed and turned for the rest of the night, unable to settle.

At 7 a.m. Sally rang to say there had been a fire in her flat in the middle of the night. The only reason she hadn't rung earlier was that since no one was hurt she hadn't wanted to disturb her sleep. Sally did not know that thanks to the psychic link mother's night's sleep had been ruined anyway.

Jean's daughter Kate, a mother of two, lives 250 miles away from her. Kate told me: 'Even when we were kids Mum would always be there the minute we opened our eyes if we were sick. Now I know if she is feeling miffed, and will give her a ring. She always knows if there is anything wrong with us. She will feel awful, and eventually Dad will get fed up of her wandering around like a lost dog and say, "For goodness sake, give the kids a ring and see which one's got the problem." We've always been a close, happy family.'

The time of giving birth is one when we feel especially linked to our own mothers. If mum is at hand to be the first visitor this can be very reassuring. Even though Ann Dewey, who now lives in Kailua, Hawaii, was thousands of miles away, her mother knew when she was in labour.

At that time Anne was living in California. Her mother was out to dinner in Ohio, 2500 miles away. Anne said: 'Right there at the dinner table Mom just laid down her fork and knew I was pushing that baby out. She felt my presence so strongly. I called her shortly after the birth to tell her the good news, and she wasn't the least bit surprised – she already knew the baby was born.

'My Mom and I are very close – as friends, not just as mother and daughter. We often pick up the phone to call each other at the same time, or write letters to each other on the same day.'

Sometimes the psychic bond can give a grown-up child a warning that it is important to go and see mum straight away and say 'I love you', because tomorrow may be too late. Sylvia, a mother with grown-up children, was ill in bed with influenza when she had an urgent feeling that she must go see her own mum who lived on the other side of Cardiff. Dragging herself out of bed she changed buses in the city centre and arrived over an hour later hot and exhausted.

'What are you doing here?' her mother asked, 'You look as if you should be in bed.' She made a fuss of Sylvia and after a happy visit Sylvia went home. The next day Sylvia's mum, who was fit and well and only in her 50s, died of a sudden heart attack.

What can we deduce from these experiences? Perhaps that it is important to keep the channels of communication open, even with the most unreasonable adolescent. When a teenager is being uncommunicative it is essential that parents use their instincts to fill in the gaps and pick up any warning signals that all may not be well. If you have a gut feeling – even if not backed up by logic – that there is a problem, tackle it with as much tact as you can. Similarly, with grown-up children it's hard – but essential – to accept them as equals, and one day perhaps as parents themselves.

Finally, remember that a mother's instincts are the ultimate secret weapon when all else fails. Listening to that inner voice can help to keep you one jump ahead of them just when it really counts.

10

Paternal Instincts

Why did I call this book *A Mother's Instincts*, and not include fathers in the title? I did find fathers who had instincts every bit as sure and sensitive as mothers, but only a small proportion of the experiences I gathered related to fathers, and even these were told to me mainly by wives or daughters.

After extensive research I have come to the conclusion that the psychic bond is predominantly a mother and child link. I can't say why for certain, but I believe it is the result of a combination of factors. Were society to make it possible and encourage a man to foster his intuitive side there would not only be more father-child psychic links but also a dramatic fall in the incidence of violence towards children within the family.

The examples I came across were often one-off incidents, although there are notable exceptions which do show that the more permanent psychic connection usually reserved for mothers can occur in fathers, particularly where the man is willing to be open and receptive (i.e. at odds with the competitive, achieving society in which we live). How many men would not be considered ridiculous for asking their boss for time off to take their child to the dentist? Or would not be asked if his wife had left him and the nanny broken both legs?

An offshoot of this is that some fathers who have psychic links with their offspring may not feel able to talk about them, unless they result in startling or dramatic events. Experiencing a sixth-sense connection with a small child runs contrary to the macho, stiff-upper-lip image still forced upon many men, especially those who wish to 'succeed' in material terms. Nappy-changing and buggy-pushing may be acceptable activities, though certainly not in working-class Britain, even today. But waking regularly in the night with the baby? That's women's stuff, isn't it?

Not according to John Helm of Friedberg in Germany, who took over what is regarded as the maternal night-waking pattern. He said: 'The birth of our first child was a nightmare. The hospital staff's "shut up and do as you're told" attitude soon turned into a "We'll teach you who's boss" stance.

'Silvia suffered serious tearing and blood loss; but there's no great loss without some small gain. In this case Silvia's loss was my gain. Since she was too weak to hold our brand new daughter the honour fell to me. Jenny spent the first two hours of her life in my arms, and she and I spent much of that time just looking at each other. I had a strong sense that a bond was forming between us, even then.

'Once home it was my duty to change Jenny's nappies and bring her to our bed for nursing at night. I was immediately struck by a strange phenomenon. Whereas I used to sleep like a log I would now awaken at night and within a minute or so hear Jenny begin to cry. This happened virtually every night for several months. I might add that Jenny slept not in our room, but in the room next door. I have a feeling that my waking like this was due to a psychic link, but I never bothered to try to "prove" my theory.

'The birth of our second child was far more pleasant. Silvia was able to hold and nurse him immediately after the birth. Although it was again my job to change and present the little bundle for nursing at night, I would not awaken until he was already crying. I suppose there is no gain without some loss.'

John Helm is not the only father to have night-waking experiences that conspire to blow conventional maternal synchronicity theories sky high. For neither in his nor the following case were the men injected with a dose of maternal hormone (which is said to have induced maternal feelings in experimental male rats).

Roger Keys-Weaver of Oregon says: 'In our family it was always

I who woke and responded when the children were in trouble in the night, not their mother, who was close to them none the less. I cannot explain why I would awaken suddenly knowing something was awry with Eric or Kevin, but on checking I found it was never a false alarm, and sometimes quite serious.'

Of course I am biased on the subject of psychic fathers, since I have seen this magical bond at work with my own husband and my middle son, Jack, and as I said in Chapter 1 it was this experience that set me on the trail of the parental sixth sense.

Of course Jack's premonition about my husband's motor cycle accident falls into the more dramatic category of psychic links. A second incident confirmed that we had a most unlikely prophet in our very down-to-earth son.

The second time, early in November 1988, turned out to be more of a prediction on Jack's part. Jack started to talk about 'a daddy with a beard' (which his had) being hit in the back of his motor bike by a lorry or van on a 'stiff' road, but that 'the daddy didn't fall off'. Like the pronouncements of all great oracles, Jack's prophecy didn't make a lot of sense at first, not even to the initiated. Then a couple of weeks later – Wednesday 30 November, 1988 to be exact – John, who was driving back from London along the M4, slowed down to match the speed of the cars ahead. The butcher's van racing up behind him, however, didn't slow down, and went into the back of John's motor cycle at about 70 m.p.h. John obligingly didn't fall off – had he done so he might well have been killed and would have ruined Jack's prophecy.

Though the experience was dramatic, there were other more everyday psychic links between John and Jack that I believe have laid the foundation for a continuing link between them.

The paternal-child link, like that between mothers and children, does seem to be rooted in close contact with the child. I am not advocating a packet of nappies and a visit to the local father-and-toddler group as the shortcut to enlightenment. The psychic bond is never that simply achieved, though it does seem from the stories I have gathered that it is based in a deep-rooted affection between father and child.

The presence of a psychic link between father and child does not of course preclude one with between mother and child. I was very in tune with Jack in spite of a bad birth experience, and this was the case for Donata Glassmeyer, whom I mentioned in Chapter 4. Her daughter Hope was, however, also very close to her father, who was involved whenever possible in her daily care. Hope and her father managed to communicate across the Atlantic, not in a dramatic life-or-death instance but for a simple message of love. Hope was at home in Ohio with her mother while her father was in Britain on a business trip. Donata says: 'One morning at exactly 2.05 a.m. (I checked the clock as I got up) Hope called me from her room. She sat bolt upright in bed, her eyes shining like headlamps. "I hear something, Momma," she said.

'Hope rarely wakes up at night. If she does, she's groggy and simply rolls over and goes back to sleep. On this particular night, however, she was quite alert, and repeated several times that she really could hear something. I reassured her and we both drifted back off to sleep.

'The next day her father called from London. He told me he had jogged that morning under a brilliant full moon. As he exercised he had asked the moon to shine her protective light down on his sleeping daughter. I confirmed the time with him. His lunar message was transmitted at exactly 7.05 London time. With the five-hour time difference her daddy's transatlantic tidings came to Hope at the precise moment she woke up.' Hope's father's psychic message outpaced Concorde.

Travel featured in several of the father-child psychic bonding experiences I came across. The stories of soldier and sailor fathers were especially fascinating, since they posed the question of a bond where there was not daily contact. But as we discovered when studying the maternal bond, constant contact with the child wasn't in itself the crucial factor. As long as the love is real and freely given by the mother it isn't the actual time you spend with the child but the closeness of that contact when you are together. Indeed, as I mentioned in Chapter 4, Rebecca Parkes had a particularly close psychic relationship with her son in spite of the fact that he spent a lot of time in the work creche. And in Chapter 1 we looked at the link between Wendy Hutton and her daughter Jo, who read her mind about wanting to see her friend Julie again. Jo's link was equally strong with her soldier father, and when she was four she managed to communicate with him and to find out when he would be coming home, even though he was on the other side of the world. Wendy told me: 'My husband was serving a six-month tour with the RAF in Belize. We expected him home in June, but in April Jo, who was four-and-a-half, disagreed with that forecast. She was adamant that her daddy would be coming home in May, and furthermore that it would be on the 23rd.

'It was several weeks later that we heard from my husband that he had been told he would be leaving Belize earlier than expected. He actually left for home on May 23rd.'

Olive French, who lives in Ryde on the Isle of Wight, had as a child not just a close emotional and physical relationship with her father but an everyday telepathy which was far stronger than that with her mother. Their relationship flourished throughout Olive's adult life and up until her father's death. Olive told me of the day many years before that her dad went away to fight in the Second World War.

'There was a special stone on the pavement in our street; the kids called it the "spitting stone" because you used to spit and make a wish as you jumped across it. I was walking up the hill and wishing when I got to the top I would see my dad walking up the other side of the hill on his way home. I knew it was impossible because my dad had gone away on a ship for months, maybe years. But I spat on the stone and wished anyway. When I got to the top of the hill I could see a figure dressed in khaki walking towards me. He was too far away to make out who he was, but I knew it couldn't be my dad. Then as the figure got nearer I began to run, calling out, "Dad, Dad." I can still remember to this day how happy I was. There had been problems with the ship, so he had been given an extra week's shore leave before he went away.'

Had Olive's father communicated telepathically with the little girl he loved so she would go and meet him? Or could a little girl's desire to see her dad again foul up ships and make time go backwards (courtesy of the spitting stone, of course)? The latter explanation is less likely than the first, but wouldn't it be nice if it were true?

We have come across many stories of mothers who have picked up on their children's distress. Gordon, who lives on the south coast of England, contacted me during a radio phone-in I was taking part in and told me the following story of a Nigerian father.

'Ten years ago I was out in Nigeria,' Gordon said, 'working as a chief engineer on a survey vessel. The crew were made up of men from different tribes. We were out in the estuary working when one of the crew, who came from a remote village many miles inland, came to me and said, "Boss, my daughter, she taken sick. I must go home." I said he could have four days' leave.

'The Captain wasn't keen, saying that there was no phone on board the ship and certainly none in the man's village, and that here we were in the middle of the creek – how could this man possibly know his daughter had been taken ill? It was just a try-on for a holiday, the Captain said. He'd probably never come back.

'But I believed the man and insisted he could go (there was much in that country I didn't understand but just accepted). After four days the man came back as promised. He told me his daughter had been taken very ill with measles and influenza, and had died the day after he returned to the village.'

As we've said, many fathers find it hard to acknowledge a psychic bond. Some fathers even have one without knowing it. Their daughter may be yelling out psychically, 'Help, Dad!', but if Dad is a bit slow on the paranormal uptake she may summon a bit of celestial help.

Jenny is a nurse, so she is not one to panic easily. She told me this story while we sat at the bedside of one of my children, who had been admitted to the local hospital. 'When my daughter Hannah was not very old, she fell over in the playground and badly shattered a tooth and hurt her face. I realized she was in no fit state to go to the dentist that day. She was very upset, but I didn't want to bother my husband at work because there wasn't anything he could do. Though he worked quite locally he never came home for lunch. This particular day, however, in he walked.

'I was amazed to see him and said, "What are you doing here? Hannah's hurt herself; I was debating whether to phone you." Hannah was delighted but not at all surprised to see her Dad. "I knew you'd come, Dad," she said, "I sent my Guardian Angel to fetch you." '

As I said, in many of the cases of paternal instinct I came across it was often a crisis or major event that sparked off the psychic link. Yet there were these other just as exciting enduring links that some men managed to maintain with their offspring. I had read in Colin Wilson's book *The Occult* (Granada, 1978) of his description of the regular telepathic links he had with his own children when they were babies. He explained that if he wanted his baby daughter to sleep through the night he had to take care not to lie awake thinking about her. If he did, she woke up. He recalls that in the case of his son he had to avoid even looking at the infant if he was asleep in his pram. 'When my wife asked me to see if he was still asleep, in the garden or on the porch, I would tiptoe to the window, glance out very quickly, then turn away. If I lingered, peering at him, he would stir and wake up. This happened so unvaryingly during his first year that I came to accept it as natural.'

Colin noted that after the first year the telepathic links seemed to snap, or at least to weaken. But once the children started to learn to speak, 'again there was a feeling – perhaps illusory – that the child could pick up and echo my own thoughts or at least respond to them when attempting to express something.'

So I wrote to Colin, who is an expert psychic researcher and author of numerous books on the paranormal, to ask him what his secret was. He confirmed what I had hypothesized: a loving, accepting relationship separated the dramatic but isolated encounters from regular psychic communication.

'I can't really remember whether telepathic links with my children began before their birth,' he told me 'but I've always had some kind of telepathic link with my wife Joy. I can remember lying in bed at night with her – when her back was to me – with my arm round her and my hand resting on her tummy, and often feeling the baby kick. I can remember Joy bringing my daughter Sally home from the hospital and handing her to me – some newspaper reporter was standing there waiting to take a photograph – and as I talked to her Sally instantly gave me the most delightful smile. From then on, of course, we were very close indeed. I can also remember saying to her quite seriously when she was a very tiny baby, only a few weeks or months old, "Do you know I think you're wonderful and I adore you?" or something of the kind, and she actually blushed. I know that sounds absurd, but I think the meaning of my words somehow got across to her.

'All three of my children – the next two were boys – were exceptionally good babies, never giving us any trouble with crying in the night even when they were teething, and I think that this was probably because they got an enormous amount of love and affection. If they showed the slightest sign of unhappiness when I was around I instantly did my best to ease it. Some parents get impatient with their children – only the other day I saw a mother dragging her screaming child out of a supermarket by one hand shouting, "Oh, do shut up," but if ours ever showed the least sign of unhappiness I instantly wanted to know what I could do to put it right. So I think this was very good for them.

'I often exploded at the children, but they understood perfectly well that it was just a temporary irritation and that two minutes later I might be puzzled that they were looking rather upset, not remembering the explosion. And I remember once we were at Disneyland and my daughter was being rather a pest. I said something like, "You little ✳✳✳, if you don't shut up, I'll jump up and down on you." The woman in front of me looked around with horror and said indignantly, "That's no way to speak to a child!" and I had to laugh because she obviously thought that I treated Sally brutally or at least indifferently all the time, whereas in fact she was so absolutely certain she was adored that it didn't matter what I said to her. So this I think explains why there was always such a strong telepathic bond between us.'

James was a teacher, and is a very gentle, caring man who finds no problem in accepting the intuitive side of his nature. He seems to illustrate the loving relationship with his children of which Colin Wilson spoke. He told me of one incident of father-child telepathy touching his everyday world. 'From 1952 to '54 we were living in Giffnock, a suburb of Glasgow, on a side road about half a mile from the main road. Before getting on the bus to go up to school I was thinking about trying to meet one of my pupils, who generally came to the nearby station, so we could go up to school together. My four-year-old daughter and I were walking up our road in silence when quite suddenly she said, "Why Giffnock station?" and then giggled because it seemed such an odd thing to say. She had certainly read my thoughts.'

The story of Rosemary from Berkshire began with a burst of love and fizzled out into coldness and indifference. Was this why Rosemary has only one precious moment of psychic connection with her father to treasure? Rosemary's communication with her father was also a long-distance call. It was towards the end of the Second World War and Rosemary's father was a sailor on the battleship HMS *Rodney* when her mother went into labour with her.

Her Dad 'knew' his wife was in labour and that the baby was a girl. He even wrote down the time and date she was born. The date was spot on (not the expected delivery date) but Rosemary thinks that the time was slightly wrong. This could of course have been due to the fact that the ship was in a different time zone.

Sadly such bonding did not extend to Rosemary's childhood. 'My Dad was away for much of my childhood, and so sadly he was a stranger and I used to resent his intruding on our lives.' But looking back, at least she felt they shared that one precious moment.

As I've said before, sometimes the magic is all there is, and maybe Rosemary's dad loved and wanted her so much that he did link in to her birth. You may only get flashes of insight if the psychic bond is not backed up on a deep physical and emotional level. The love may be there, but some men still have problems showing it to their children.

It's not only dads who can't be home a lot who have this problem. Men can lose contact in other ways, by becoming over-involved in work, sport or hobbies, afraid – even if they see their child every day – to open up their souls and expose their own vulnerability to the infant. If the 'new' gentle, caring man is to become a reality, maybe it is in the nursery that he can begin to learn to listen to his intuitive side.

Divorce is also very common, and too often a father may lose contact with his children. Again, however, it's not constant contact that is vital, but even a closeness during time shared together can be difficult for the absent parent to maintain. While I was reading through some old records of the Alister Hardy Research Centre in Oxford, I came across a letter from a divorced American father written many years ago about the telepathic link between himself and his daughter.

Thomas wrote: 'It happened in Culver City, California, about the first week in December. I arose one Saturday morning – and reminded myself that some time before the stores closed that day

I must buy my daughter Shirley the doll her mother had told me she wanted for Christmas. Her mother and I were divorced, and Shirley was living with her mother in San Fernando. That morning as I thought about my ex-wife and my child I cried like a baby. After my tears were dried, I sat staring at a small spot on the rug, alone with my thoughts.

'That is all I remember until I returned to consciousness after what at first seemed to be only a few minutes later. But I noticed that it was dark outside, and when I looked at my watch I could hardly believe my eyes: it was 6 p.m.! I had been sitting in that chair for almost ten hours. After recovering from this shock, the first thought which entered my mind was that I must hurry and get dressed and go buy that doll for Shirley before the stores closed. I quickly drove to the nearest department store.

'I went up to the toy department and found a showcase where several dolls were on display. I immediately saw the doll my ex-wife had told me Shirley wanted. I did not like it. In fact I thought it was very ugly. I then looked at some of the other dolls, and noticed one dressed in white. I thought this doll was pretty. Since there was no clerk in the immediate vicinity I turned to a counter about six feet away which had some toys on display. I picked up a doctor's kit and examined it carefully; I thought it was one of the best toys of that type which I had ever seen. I set it back on the counter, then turned back to the display with the pretty doll dressed in white. Then I turned again to look at the doctor's kit. Back and forth I went, in great haste, eight or ten times. I shall never forget the feeling I experienced. I remember it vividly; it seemed like I was propelled between those two objects as though between the poles of a magnet. I was deeply puzzled by my actions.

'In the meantime a couple came along and picked up the doctor's kit which I had looked at. They took it and left to go pay for it. There were only two on display, and I went over and picked up the remaining one. On examining it I discovered it was broken. Shortly after this a saleslady came by, and I said to myself,

"Oh well, I don't like the doll that Shirley wants but if that is what she wants I will buy it for her." I purchased the doll and then asked the saleslady if she could find another doctor's kit like the one on the counter which was broken. She looked around but said it was the last item of that kind in stock. It was now almost time for the store to close, and I left somewhat disappointed.

'The following afternoon, Sunday, I called my ex-wife and told her that I wanted to come over and bring Shirley her doll. She said they'd be in all day, so I took the doll and went over to their house. As I got there my ex-wife said, laughing, "Tom, the funniest thing happened last night. I took Shirley to see Santa Claus. She wanted to tell him about the doll and the other things she wants for Christmas. When she was sitting on his lap I never saw her act so strange. It seemed she could not make up her mind, and do you know what she finally asked Santa Claus to bring her? Not the doll she liked so much before. She told him she wanted a bridal doll and a doctor's kit. I think it is so strange," she continued, "because she had never mentioned anything about a bridal doll or a doctor's kit before." "What's a bridal doll?" I asked.

' "Oh, don't be silly," she replied, "You know, a doll dressed in white like a bride."

'It was at this instant that I decided to go back to the department store to see if the doll in white was still there. If it was I would note whether it was dressed like a bride or not. Then I asked my ex-wife the approximate time she took Shirley to see Santa Claus the previous evening. "Oh, I don't know," she said, "somewhere about eight or nine o'clock, I suppose." I didn't say anything to my ex-wife about my experience the night before at approximately the same time.

'After I finished work on Monday I returned to the department store. The same doll was still in the showcase. It was indeed dressed like a bride. I immediately purchased the doll, and then decided to look for a doctor's kit on my way to San Fernando.

I was able to purchase one not far from where Shirley and my ex-wife lived. When I got to their house I told my ex-wife about my experience on Saturday night. "Telepathy," she laughed, then quickly changed the subject.

'I doubt if she remembers the episode today. Anyway, that is how my daughter Shirley happened to receive a doll dressed in white and a doctor's kit for Christmas.'

Thomas would now be about 80, and his daughter grown up, perhaps with her own family. I failed to trace them but the story has haunted me. Did Thomas get to know his daughter as she grew older? If Thomas is alive, are they still in touch? Or was this incident the last or perhaps the only link between them? If so it is doubly precious, and serves as a reminder that the magic of the psychic bond lies in the potential fulfilment it holds for the relationship. How many people sit alone with old photographs and sad or bitter memories? I hope Thomas' story had a happy ending. I should love to know.

How can we foster the deep psychic link in our own families? Fatherhood is one of the few times in their lives when men are given an opportunity to unfold and develop their intuitive, protective, caring nature. This is easier for some men than others, and may not happen naturally. Your resident male can initially – though he'd never admit it in the pub or to the football team – feel a bit displaced by this new rival for your adoration. If this is the case he should be thrown in at the deep end. Arm him with a packet of nappies (the instructions, being intended for mothers, are remarkably simple) and a bottle of milk, and leave father and infant to get on with the bonding. You may find you're the one a bit miffed when you return to find the mutual adoration society of father and child. Afterwards the psychic bonds will flow along with everything else, and are a good foundation for a truly happy family. You are sowing the seeds for a gentler kind of man in the real world. And that, given the conflict and violence both in the family and society, can be no bad thing.

Death is the ultimate separation for parent and child. But even then the closeness of paternal love need not end. For Doris, who is now in her 80s, her dad's funeral when she still a little girl was anything but a solemn affair. 'I was always very close to my Dad,' she told me. 'He was always laughing and joking, and we used to know what the other was thinking. When he died I was totally lost. But even at the funeral my dad managed to cheer me up. We lived in Croydon at the time. I can still remember as if it were yesterday. All the relatives were crying and wearing black. I knew Dad would have hated all that fuss.

'We were standing at the graveside when suddenly I looked up and there was dad in the sky, grinning and waving at me like mad. I just burst out laughing – I was so pleased to see him. Of course I got into trouble afterwards because I'd laughed, but I didn't care; I knew my dad was still there looking after me.'

Was it a little girl's imagination, or was her father's love so strong that he couldn't bear to see her sad? But this wasn't the last time Doris' dad called her up on the psychic hotline. Doris told me: 'I was in my 20s and I was walking up Clapham High Street. Though I say it myself, I thought I looked a bit of a treat. Suddenly who should I bump into but my dad. I was so shocked, I just stood there. "Hello gel," he said, "you've put on a bit of weight round your hips."'

11

Adoptive Parents

Lorraine had the classic pre-birth dream: it correctly predicted the sex and looks of her child. But there was one big difference: her son Ivan was adopted.

The dream, which she recorded in her journal, was of a blonde-haired, fair-skinned woman giving birth to a dark-skinned, black-haired infant. At the time she thought the woman in the dream was her pregnant next-door neighbour. Months later, Lorraine and her husband were offered a mixed-race baby born of a white woman. Lorraine was startled to discover that Ivan had been born at the same hour she had had her dream, and that she had awakened at the moment of his birth.

Incidents like this rather overthrow the idea that the mother-child bond might be a totally genetic link. And they are not uncommon according to Rita Laws, who has researched the bond between adoptive parents and children extensively. She has also had a great deal of personal experience of the 'adoptive' bond, having seven adopted children as well as three birthchildren (in Chapter 1 I described how she shared psychic toothaches with her own son and her adopted one). She is also president of the Oklahoma branch of AASK (the Association for the Aid to Adoption of Special Kids) and editor of the AASK newsletter *ADD-OPTION*.

Rita sees the psychic link between parents and children as very important in aiding the bonding process between adoptive parents and their new offspring.

'Adoptive parents tend to be, understandably, a bit more insecure about their role, at least at first. Psychic phenomena during and after the adoption process are a valuable source of confirmation of a bond between them and their new child. We feel a bit more secure in our roles as parents when we can point to an unexplainable event, an impossible coincidence, that somehow validates the match. Eventually this insecurity fades entirely, helped along in part by the continuing and growing psychic link. Just as biological parents do, adoptive parents find themselves waking up moments before the baby does, or jumping up when the child, playing in the next room, hurts himself. Even though this link grows more slowly than it does for birthparents, in the end it is just as strong. The bonding catches up to the parent and child if they are patient and loving with one another.

'Our first adopted son, Tony, was born in February of 1984. Our third birthchild, Joaquin, was born exactly seven-and-a-half months later. When he in turn was seven-and-a-half months old I joked to my husband that it was time for another baby, but even as I joked I had an overwhelming sense that we would have three sons born exactly seven-and-a-half months apart. We then applied to adopt a girl, but were offered a son instead. Jesse, adopted in July, 1985, was born in May, 1985, exactly seven-and-a-half months after Joaquin.

'I was able to breast-feed both Tony and Jesse even though they were not born to me. Jesse and I had every bit as close a link as I had with any of my other children; and when it came to sleeping our link was the closest. For the first five years of his life (he is now five-and-a-half) he always woke when I did. He slept with me till he was three, but even once he was in a different bedroom he would also wake up within five minutes of me. I used to think this was because of the breast-feeding, but he did this even after weaning. It is only recently that he has begun, sometimes, to sleep later than I do.'

Adoptive parents commonly look for omens – even those who don't believe in signs, says Rita. 'The most common scenario is the adoptive mother who knows that her future child has just been born – months or weeks before hearing about the child.'

Lorraine's dream about Ivan, her second adopted child, can be taken as a very strong omen. She also had a sign with Karen, her first adopted child. Karen was several months old when Lorraine and her husband first heard about her, but she had been born, coincidentally, the same week they decided to try to adopt a child. Lorraine likes to think of this as a sign or a confirmation that the adoption was meant to be.

Dr Lauren Bradway is an adoptive mother from Oklahoma who has also studied the adoptive bond. She too felt a strong pre-adoptive link with her daughter. 'I had a dream one night that my daughter was born and was reassuring me she was on the way. Exactly sixteen months later we received a call from the adoption agency saying that they had a little girl for us. Then they told me her birthdate – it was the night of my dream.'

Barbara and Dave have five adopted children. Their third child, a bi-racial infant daughter, was no surprise to Barbara when they first met because she had seen Darlene clearly in a daytime vision long before the adoption.

Their first adopted child was born on the very day they tried to adopt (after four years of marriage). Barbara says that parental psychic phenomena are part of a primitive survival mechanism, just as necessary to the survival of adopted children as children in any other situation.

Rita remembers a symbolic experience before the adoption of her first child that is comparable to the pre-birth premonitions of mothers. She and her husband first applied to adopt a child in September. At Christmas Rita's husband took her to buy the birthstone ring she had always wanted. But at the last minute she changed her mind and asked for an aquamarine, the birthstone for March. For two months she wore the ring, wondering why it seemed so important to her. For reasons Rita was at a loss to explain, the ring symbolized an 'event' she was sure would change her life forever. Six months sooner than expected, on 12 March, the adoption agency rang. Rita and her husband picked up their son two days later. Since then Rita has adopted six other children, and is very involved in the work of the adoption of children with special needs. So March, as the ring suggested, was the birth of a very important phase of her life.

In Chapter 7 while discussing reincarnation I mentioned the theory that unborn children might try to choose the mother they wanted to be born to. By extension, could unborn children choose their adoptive parents? If they could then Rita's second adopted child, Jesse, would certainly deserve a medal for prenatal determination. He positively chased his hesitant parents. 'When we were ready to adopt in 1985,' Rita told me, 'we contacted my tribe, the Choctaw Indians of Oklahoma, the Native American Adoption Resource Exchange in Pennsylvania (NAARE), a private agency and the state adoption agency. We asked for a girl, preferably younger than our eldest child, who was five, and we were open accepting a child with disabilities. We were firm about not wanting another boy (our daughter wanted a sister) and about not wanting another infant (we had two). The tribe called in March and described Jesse, who was not even going to be born for two months, as half-Black, half-Choctaw, gender unknown and paternity unknown. We sadly declined because, male or female, this was an infant. We couldn't see it as fair to deprive another person of an infant when we had already had that pleasure.

'In May, NAARE called. They had matched us to a newborn Oklahoma baby, half-Black, half-Choctaw – the same one the tribe had called us about.

'Again we declined reluctantly. In June, the private agency called and offered us the same baby! In July, we called the tribe and asked for the child, convinced by now that he was meant to be our son. But the tribe no longer had custody of Jesse. They had turned him over to the state, which was now trying to find him a family. I called the state and asked for the social worker who had known us for several years. She immediately said she had been going to phone us that day to offer us a child. When I described the child to her she was amazed. "How did you know?" she asked over and over.

'Three days later Jesse was home. Later we found out he was born in Shawnee, Oklahoma, just like our second child, Tim. Jesse had also been delivered by the same doctor who delivered Tim. A year later I obtained a photograph of Jesse's birthmother, and was surprised to see she was wearing the exact same wristwatch I have. One more thing – Jesse's initials before adoption were LAW – similar to my last name.'

A series of coincidences or something more profound which we cannot understand? Perhaps it is most important to bear in mind that whatever the reason, the experience helped to create a link between Rita and Jesse which, as she has said, was every bit as close as that she shares with any of her other children, despite her initial reluctance to adopt him.

Rita says: 'Several of my friends have, like me, adopted both infants and older kids as well as having given birth. We tend to agree that eventually the frequency of psychic events and the intensity of bonding is no different between adopted and biological infants, and also that omens and signs are very important parts of this bonding process, because they confirm the rightness of the adoption. However, the bonding between the adopted parent and the older child is unique and different in that you are friends first and then you become parent and child. Still the psychic link is there, growing stronger over time, although because the child is older the frequency of happenings may be much lower.'

In the case of Rita's sixth adopted child, the maternal instinct helped her to bond him to her in circumstances that might have proved traumatic for both the foster mother, Rita herself, and most importantly the child.

'Jamie was two years and 11 months old when we adopted him, and though very delayed in development he was still old enough to be very attached to his foster mother – the only mom he had ever known. For some reason I had tacked up his photo on the wall, though he wasn't the only child nor necessarily the most likely child we would end up with (there were several other possibilities). When the social worker telephoned to say he would become our son, I was looking at Jamie's photo on the wall. I was delighted but very worried he wouldn't want to leave his foster mother and come with us. Then I had a dream in which Jamie came with us willingly because his foster mother gave him verbal permission to love us. Strange as it sounds I decided to try that approach, because I believed the dream was giving me an answer to a potentially very distressing situation (where logic had failed).

'So I flew to the big and totally unfamiliar city of Baltimore and attempted to drive across a couple of counties to meet my son (my husband was to meet me the next day). In spite of excellent directions I became hopelessly lost in my rented car, time and time again. Finally, late in the afternoon I called the social worker from a phone booth at the height of rush-hour traffic, tears of frustration streaming down my cheeks. In spite of my pleas she refused to come and get me, instead telling me to calm down and "come meet your son". I did calm down and concentrated on homing in on Jamie, deciding to go where my heart led me. As I approached different highway junctions and exits I consulted my map and also consulted my inner radar. I arrived quickly at my destination in spite of construction detours, without any further problems. Jamie stuck close to his mom and pretty well ignored me during that visit, but I loved him deeply immediately.

'I returned with my husband Amado the next day, and we helped the foster mom pack Jamie's things. At this point he figured out he had to go with us and began crying and screaming and clinging to his foster mom, a very common scenario. I asked her to speak to Jamie in our presence, even though he probably wouldn't understand much, and explain that it was all right for him to go with us. I tried to explain to Jamie's foster mother that I "knew" Jamie would understand in his heart, even if her words seemed incomprehensible. But she refused, and fighting back tears demanded that we just go, take him and go (she had not been able to adopt him herself due to health problems). I picked up Jamie and we got as far as the front door when he began kicking and screaming hysterically. My heart was heavy because I knew this was the worst possible way to begin our relationship.

'But as I stepped outside, the foster mom suddenly changed her mind, called us back in and took Jamie from me. She sat down on the settee, put Jamie on her lap and smiled at him. Then she told him it was OK to love us because we loved him as much as she did. She promised to always love him and to be his grandma and write him letters. Then she told him to go with us and not to worry about anything. It happened just as I had seen in my dream. Jamie immediately stopped crying and looked at me as if he was seeing me for the very first time. He held out his arms to me and said, "Go bye-bye now". He left with us quite happily, racing us out to the car, and he did not cry, not one little bit. In fact he did not cry for two weeks after the adoption, and only cried then because he fell off the swing in the yard and bumped his knee.

'To this day he looks at photos of his foster mom, calls her Grandma and seems perfectly content. I always feel like I saw a miracle that day. I believe the psychic bond to be of a protective nature. My maternal heart, knowing that Jamie could be potentially traumatized by the adoption, found a way to protect him and conveyed one possible solution to me via a dream. I wonder if Jamie had dreamed a similar dream, making the real life event familiar to him as a sort of *déjà vu* experience?'

The experiences of Rita and others with adopted children seem to suggest that a mother's instincts can be felt by anyone occupying a mothering role for a child. I believe the parent-child link does not depend entirely on genetics and is not exclusive to birth mothers. The strangest thing is, however, that although separated by perhaps thousands of miles and 20 years or more, a child can still retain some psychic link with his or her birthmother even though he or she might never have known the woman.

This link can manifest itself in subtle ways. For instance, Barbara and Dave's adopted child Darlene, now aged 5, does not know that she was originally named Louise, but she has named every doll she has ever had Louise.

This memory of a name the child never knew is particularly significant, says Dr LaVonne Stiffler of Florida, who has studied the intuitive links between adopted children and their natural parents from whom they were separated at birth. 'Whether or not the birthmother officially named her baby,' says Dr Stiffler, 'each mother knows the name by which she will remember this life, and carries it with her in unspoken prayer, bringing it to her conscious mind on the child's birthday, anniversary of the adoption or other significant occasions.'

One adopted child told her: 'When I was a little girl and all through my teenage years I always wanted to be called Maggie. Not for any particular reason, I just always wanted that name. When I located my original name in the state's birth register, I found that it was Margaret. So I really was a Maggie all along.'

Occasionally the name-bond can work in reverse, as one mother recalled. 'I had sent for and received records from the hospital where I had given birth to my son 25 years before. Also enclosed were a copy of his footprints. The footprints were what really got to me emotionally. I wrote a poem about him that day and superimposed copies of his little footprints on it. I thumbtacked it to the wall just inside my bedroom door. A few months later I walked into my bedroom to get ready for bed. I glanced at the tiny footprints again. At that moment the name Bryan appeared in my thoughts, out of nowhere. I felt somewhat shaken. I decided it had to be the name given to him by his adoptive parents, and when we were reunited I discovered his name was indeed Bryan.'

Dr Stiffler's work for her doctorate for the Oxford Graduate School in Dayton, Tennessee was unique in that parent-child intuition had only previously been studied in relation to children who were raised with their families. She studied 70 sets of parents and children who had been separated by the social and legal practice of secret, stranger adoption who had been reunited when the children were adults after a lengthy search. Most of them were residents of the United States and were studied between May 1990 and May 1991.

She herself experienced strange links with the child she had been forced to give away many years before. She says that in many cases when the reunited mother and child begin to piece together the years of their separation they find not only mutual physical characteristics and personal mannerisms but also 'incidents of intuition and synchronicity, suggesting a continuance of the prenatal bond'.

Dr Stiffler sees this link as beyond our current understanding of genetics. 'The memory of a lullaby may have originated pre-natally. But whence come the vivid dreams, the naming of an imaginary playmate or the strange feeling of being drawn to a particular location?'

The search for each other is also an area where strange 'homing' instincts seem to operate. Dr Stiffler comments: 'The migratory and homing behaviours of animals have been admired, yet remain mysterious to humanity. Should there be any less marvellous a programme for an adoptee's homing instinct than that designed for the Alaskan salmon?'

One woman said: 'I had been searching for my mother for a year and getting nowhere. One day at work a co-worker asked if I was having any luck. Another woman who worked there overheard us and asked, "Luck about what?" I took out my birth certificate and the woman said, "I might know someone who can help." She asked me for a baby picture and took it home to compare it with one she had. She was my mother. She had been trying to find me for nearly 20 years, always running into dead ends. We live in a large city of around 230,000 people, and I had started working at this store just a few days before she did. The other girl we worked with was raised by my birthfather. She knew exactly where he was. So, all in one day, I found my mother and knew where my father was, too. And I had been living just three streets away from my mother for nearly three years.'

Dr Stiffler found that death seemed a strong trigger for a psychic link which might have lain dormant for years. One woman recalled: 'When I was nine I demanded another sister from my adoptive parents. They duly adopted another girl. I have since found out that my real sister was orphaned at this time. Our mother died and she had no one and so was put into welfare homes. I believe I knew the day my mum died as I had an uncontrollable outburst one day. My anger was extreme and I nearly killed a friend of mine.'

Another woman said: 'I was an adoptee who found some of my maternal family 10 years ago. My birthmother was deceased by the time I found them. One of the first things I asked was, "When did she die?" When they told me I found I could remember that day very well; I had written in my journal, "I feel someone close to me has died." '

Dr Stiffler also discovered that in times of crisis mother and child, though separated shortly after the birth, respond to each other's distress. Said one: 'I kept a diary before our reunion and I wrote in it about the time my daughter was 15 that I felt unusually upset about our separation. When we were reunited, she told me that when she was 15 she had run away and tried to find me, to no avail.'

Another birthmother told Dr Stiffler: 'When my daughter was 13 years old I found myself thinking about her constantly. I felt that if I was with her things would be different. That is the year I decided that someday, somehow I would find her. I later found out that that was the year she had lost her virginity to an older man and was having great problems with her family.'

Was it an early memory of the few months mother and child were together or instinct that prepared one adopted daughter to meet her mother many years later? This young woman told Dr Stiffler that she had always sensed that a piece of her life's puzzle was missing. 'Throughout my life I was always triggered by an interest in sign language, so I learned it from friends and people in my church.' When she finally located her mother they first exchanged letters and pictures. Then they arranged a reunion. She met her mother at the airport, and as she did she lifted her hands in a gesture which 'God had been preparing me for without my knowing why'. Her mother was deaf, and understood her sign – the one beautiful word she had waited years to express: 'Mother'.

Just as separated twins have unexplained links in their lives, so too, according to Dr Stiffler, have mothers and children who have been apart. 'My daughter and I were both in bike accidents in 1971,' one mother remembered. 'She fell off her bike and broke her front tooth and I went flying over my bike and broke my front tooth. When she told me she had a cap on her front tooth, I said, "So do I." '

Another mother said: 'One year I absolutely had to buy a particular short, dark green corduroy jacket with a hood. It also came in burgundy. I have learned that my daughter in the same year insisted, even though her folks were poor, that she must have the same jacket in burgundy. We both had acted entirely out of our normal patterns, with a frantic desire to have the coat. After our reunion, when I was giving my daughter some of my old clothes, she squealed when she saw the jacket.'

What then can we learn from this adoptive psychic bond? First that love and magic are not open to simple or even complex explanations. Birthmothers do seem to keep links with their children even when they are separated from them and have no idea where they are. But then we never forget the children we lose, be it through giving them up for adoption or through death, for they are always a part of us. It is doubtful whether any genetic pattern could explain how a child could choose a jacket identical to the one the mother she never knew has chosen, or how a mother could come off her bike and break her front tooth in the same year as the child she had no contact with. Coincidences? Similarly, are the bonds between adoptive mothers and their adopted offspring signs that the relationship is right and permanent?

As I have said before, yes, there is magic, and it is a magic that can help an adopted child feel he didn't just spring from nowhere. But it is important that the everyday intuitive links aren't cast aside in favour of the other, magical ones. If birthmothers and separated children are to be reunited both must be helped to establish a realistic bond; it will need to be rebuilt slowly.

Because the bond is not exclusive, a child doesn't need to renounce his adopted parents who have inch-by-inch built up not only a psychic but physical relationship. But as Dr Stiffler points out, there is a need for further research into how birthmothers can be helped not only through the lifelong trauma of giving a child up for adoption but also as to how reunions can be managed so that the high hopes, based sometimes on these magical intuitions, don't come crashing down. Until then we shall have to rely on our own instincts to protect children and both birth and adoptive mothers in this most sensitive area of human and psychic experience.

12

Beyond Motherhood

Do you have a psychic link with snotty-nosed Johnny down the road? Perhaps, if you have been taking care of him after school while mum is working and, despite his runny nose, are very much in sympathy with his needs. For as we saw with adoptive bonds, the psychic link with a child does not necessarily spring from a blood tie (though the sweat and tears are obligatory). A child's primary bond is of course with his mother, though some fathers who are particularly sensitive and caring have cracked it, too. But it can also extend to other family members and occasionally to other people involved in the child's care, such as childminders.

This 'non-family' bond is a reflection of our changing world. In the days of the extended family, when children were cared for by grannies and aunties on a regular basis if mum was absent, the bond would have been largely home-based. But with paid help or neighbours taking the place of the old support network, the psychic bond has had to adapt – and has done so remarkably well.

One regular babyminder's 'psychic link' with the small child she cared for enabled her to save his life. The late American theological writer Catherine Marshall recalled a woman who was very attached to the baby she regularly cared for, and who saved his life by following what seemed to be a sudden irrational urge. Lynne usually left her 11-month-old son Brandon in the care of her good friend Ginny, but one weekend in 1972 Ginny was unavailable so Lynne left the baby with her sister Nancy instead. The baby was teething and restless, so by the Sunday Nancy decided to move the cot from the guest room to the play room down the hall, so that she could hear him when he cried.

That evening Ginny arrived to say: 'I've come to take Brandon with me.' When Nancy protested, Ginny explained: 'Lynne had asked me to keep Brandon. I was the one who should have taken him but we had something on for the weekend.' Nancy was hesitant at first but Ginny insisted, so Nancy eventually agreed and Ginny drove off with the baby. Later that night Nancy's house caught fire. The blaze started in the playroom, just a few feet from where the baby would have been sleeping. There would have been no way of getting him out alive.

Ginny told Nancy afterwards that she had been restless all that particular Sunday afternoon. Her thoughts kept going to Brandon. The child was obviously all right with Nancy, but Ginny suddenly had the strong feeling she must go and bring him back to her house. She was afraid it would sound silly so she tried to shake off the feeling, but by dinner time she knew she had to fetch the child.

Catherine Marshall cited this as a case of 'divine intervention'. For those who are religious such experiences can be seen in this way, and such a view in no way negates the idea of unspoken bonds between parent or carer and child. But even without a theological explanation, the positive, caring nature of these instincts, whatever terminology we use, are paramount. But again, as we found with the paternal bond, these experiences tend to be isolated rather than continual.

William's grandad wasn't his real grandad at all but an elderly neighbour who used to pick him up from school and amuse him when William's parents were busy. Then William developed a rare form of cancer. When his parents realized William did not have long to live, they took him to Majorca for a special holiday. As soon as they got home William rushed down the road to tell 'Grandad' what a great holiday he had had. 'Would you like to go to Majorca?' William asked him. 'It's brilliant.'

'I wish I could,' the old man replied, 'but I couldn't afford it.'

Not long after this conversation William's condition deteriorated rapidly, and he died a few weeks later. After his death a raffle was held to further research into childhood cancers. Thousands of tickets were sold. The prize was an all-expenses-paid holiday to Majorca. When the raffle was drawn, William's 'grandad' won the holiday. Was it a coincidence, or William's way of saying thank you to his surrogate grandfather?

Step-parents have got a bad press from Hansel and Gretel onwards, and no one would see step-parenting as an easy role. It is not like adoption, since the child may find that suddenly one familiar parent is replaced by a total stranger – it can be a no-win situation for step-parent and child, and not one where we would expect the psychic bond to flourish, certainly not on the everyday basis that we find with mothers and some fathers.

Yet for Veronica, who is now in her late 40s and living in the south of England, her relationship with her step-father not only became the central one of her life, but it was with him and not her mother that the psychic bonds were formed. The relationship did not begin well, however. 'I was still quite young when my step-father arrived in my life, and at first I resented having to share my mother. But soon he became the pivot of my life. Whenever I needed him he was there for me, and no words were necessary. Once when I was quite young I fell at school and hurt my leg very badly. In those days it was safe to come home by yourself in the country, even quite long distances, and so I always walked the mile home by myself. But my step-dad just knew I couldn't make it this one day, and so he came to meet me and carried me home.

'Another day he was hammering away in his shed. He hit his thumb and it went black. As I came in from school, I realized my thumb was really tender. I told my mother my thumb was hurting, though I hadn't done anything to it. "You'd better join your father, then," she said, "he's just hit his thumb with the hammer." Because of the very close relationship between us, I could always tell how he was feeling or pick up on his pain.

'When I was a bit older and taking exams Dad would see me out of the door in the morning, and as I sat chewing my pen in the examination room he would come visually into my mind and I would be calmed.

'The bond lasted even after childhood. I was in my 20s when he died, but I suddenly knew Dad was dead, though I was on the other side of the world. I was convinced he had died, but I couldn't just ring up and ask Mum, "Has Dad died?" – it seemed so stupid. Then about an hour later our family doctor rang from Britain and said he had bad news.

'The bonds between us didn't cease even then, though. He was still always there, in his practical, caring, calming way. Whenever I was in trouble I would smell his special aroma – woodsmoke and clean shirts – and know he was there helping me.

'I was in Khartoum during the civil war there. My husband had had to go south and I didn't know what would happen to him. There was no radio and no telephone, and I was at the end of my tether. I was half-crying. Suddenly I smelled Dad's special aroma and could hear him telling me – just as he used to when I was a little girl and was moaning I couldn't manage something – "Quit whining and get on with it. You'll not solve the problem by sitting there feeling sorry for yourself. Do something about it."

'So I got the children and the truck ready for a hasty departure. I don't know what would have happened if Dad hadn't calmed me down. Without my step-father I might have gone through my whole life without being that close to anyone. Strangely enough he had children from a previous marriage but he never saw them. With us, it was a uniting of kindred spirits.'

The qualities of the relationship between Veronica and her step-father were those we found in the closest parent-and-child bonds: gentle, practical, consistent care during the time they spent together. And it is strange that the bonds with his own children were not as close. But this continuous psychic link between non-family members is still rare.

Some children today do still enjoy the more conventional

family network where they are cared for by other relatives as well as their mother on a regular basis. This structure is still the norm in more traditional societies, such as the Hindu culture. Here the birth of a child is still a family event, and female relatives can be very involved emotionally and psychically even in the baby's early weeks.

Shirley Firth, the expert in Indian studies, told me of an experience she had recorded in which a dead child returned to see not his mother but his aunt, his father's sister. Shirley told me: 'An Indian woman lost a baby when he was only one week old. Immediately after the child's death the infant appeared to her sister-in-law in a dream and said, "My mother gave me everything but she did not give me bananas. If you bring me bananas, I will come again." The sister-in-law told the baby's mother of the dream and his mother took bananas to the Temple of the Mother Goddess. Within a month she was pregnant again. She believes it is her child come again.'

A British woman told me of an experience with her nephew, whom she had never seen and who'd been born to a sister she barely knew. Angela and her sister had been separated at birth. Angela is now in her 20s and lives on the Isle of Wight, while her sister ended up in Holland where she married and had a son. Eventually they contacted each other and exchanged letters and photos. Angela was looking forward to meeting her nephew, then 18 months old, when one evening she suddenly felt that there was something wrong with him. She felt he was in his room in his cot and was running a high fever, and that he was too ill to cry. 'I could see him lying there and I felt very feverish, as though I was picking up his illness. I didn't even have my sister's phone number, so I tried International Directory Inquiries and at last got through. She was very surprised to hear from me and very annoyed when I told her that she must go and check the baby at once as he had a high temperature – I used to have them as a child. "The baby always sleeps through," she insisted, "and hasn't made a sound. He would have cried if he was ill. If I go in, I'll wake him up."

'I could tell she thought I was off my trolley, but I kept insisting she check the baby. At last she rang off, saying she would, but I knew she thought I was just interfering. But it was lucky I insisted, because when she went into his room the baby was very hot indeed, and too ill to cry. She phoned the doctor, who said it was a sudden virus and admitted the baby to hospital overnight. He recovered, but had she not gone into his room when she did, who knows what would have happened?

'When she rang me the next day to thank me and say the baby would be all right, she asked me how I could possibly have known as I'd never even met the child. I don't know the answer, except that when I saw his photo I had felt very close to him.'

This does not mean that the natural parents – like Veronica's mother or Angela's sister – were in any way bad parents; but here we have instances of the rare occasions when the psychic bond seems to flow more easily between the child and someone other than his parents. It's impossible to say why this should be so while we know so little about these elusive instincts. For example, who can say why Lesley Westrum's brother should have had a premonition about her unborn child? Lesley, who is from Wisconsin, told me about her fourth child Rachel Elizabeth. 'She is red-haired, blue-eyed, and like her older sister was born on the date she was due. At first we couldn't decide on a name, so we made lists and finally settled on Rachel Elizabeth. A week later we took her to the church to be blessed. My brother, who lived in the southern part of the state, asked what we'd decided to name the baby. When we told him the name we'd finally decided on, he pulled his datebook from his pocket and showed me an entry. Some time before he'd had a dream; in it had been told that his sister would bear a daughter, Rachel Elizabeth. He wanted to be sure we'd spelled Elizabeth "right" – with a z, none of this trendy Elisabeth stuff. And her names weren't that common, like Debbie, Kathy or Jennifer.'

In Westernized society the traditional apple-cheeked white-haired granny, baking cookies and dispensing words of wisdom and comfort, might be regarded as an archetype of the caring relationship, all unspoken reassurance and intuitive anticipation of a grandchild's every need. The modern granny, however, having thrown off her own maternal responsibilities with some relief, is more likely to head for the open road. Any wisdom will be dispensed on the backs of postcards from exotic places. Peggy Rouse, although a career woman, maintains close, intuitive links with her grandchildren. She described to me an incident concerning her five-year-old granddaughter, Charlotte.

'One of my daughters and her two children were coming to stay in July. About two hours before they were due to arrive I got a towel from the airing cupboard and started twisting it around the handles of the lavatory doorknob. Jo, another of my daughters, asked me what on earth I was doing. "I must tie up this door so that it can't shut, or Charlotte will get her hand caught in it," I remember replying.

'Just at that moment the telephone rang. Jo answered it and it was my daughter saying, "We'll be at least an hour late. Charlotte has just shut her hand in the lavatory door and has no skin on her fingers." That happened in Kent; I was in Wiltshire.'

Peggy has very strong views on children, and her sensitive, totally unsentimental and empathic approach towards them are perhaps key in her close bonding with her grandchildren. 'Don't talk to children, listen to them,' she told me. She believes that children are highly evolved animals showing spiritual instincts. Parents rapidly set about de-spiritualizing them to create mercenary humanized creatures in their own image. At about three-and-a-half years old children tend to shed their spiritual aura almost like a snake shedding its skin. To Peggy children are full-blown people, not to be patronized or talked down to but treated with the respect and dignity that should be accorded to everyone. 'Perhaps it is when a child is three-and-a-half that some parents win the battle. The terrible twos are probably the child's last effort at clinging to his or her own image before surrendering to parent power,' she says.

'I always bonded with my grandchild Charlotte, right from the start. From when she was about five months old I would read to her and talk to her and she would respond, holding my fingers and working them as I spoke. I remember when Charlotte was ten months old she was sitting in her highchair and we were chatting away as usual – we had such fun. My son-in-law, bemused, asked me, "How do you know what she is saying? I can't understand a word." But of course I did. Charlotte and I always had wonderful conversations. And naturally we can read each other's thoughts. It has always happened with my own daughters, so there is nothing strange in it – it is part of an incredibly close and mutually supportive relationship. But usually it shows up in simple ways. For example, once when she was about five Charlotte was staying with me and we were driving along in the car. I was wondering what we could have for dinner that evening. I thought "There's a chicken in the deep freezer." At that moment Charlotte piped in "And I'm going to stuff it with tarragon because I always stuff chickens with tarragon at Gran's".'

So why is Peggy able to maintain the kind of everyday close links usually reserved for the maternal link? Because she gives to her grandchildren not continuous but nevertheless close, accepting care when she *is* with them. We found with the paternal bond that it was this closeness of spiritual and emotional contact, not the amount of actual time spent together, that determined whether the dramatic, one-off psychic link carried over into the everyday world. As with Veronica's step-father, Peggy has tuned in to her grandchild's wavelength and can appreciate her perspective.

The psychic bond is not however always a comfortable one, nor can it be lied to. Sometimes the clarity of a child's vision can cut through the fictions that can be woven into family life. This can have the effect of clearing away old deceptions and forcing everyone to accept healthy if uncomfortable home truths. The psychic bond is one that thrives on honesty and openness. Such was the case for young Chris.

This story begins during World War Two, when teenaged Josie fell pregnant by a serviceman who stayed briefly in her town in the south of England. There was no question of marriage, so Josie's baby was passed off as her brother. Phil was in his late teens before he was told of his true relationship to his 'sister'. The revelation had a freezing effect on their relationship and caused great deal of heartache in the family. Later Phil left home, got married and in due course had a son of his own, which somewhat healed the family breach. From the earliest age, however, Phil's little boy, Chris, insisted on calling Josie 'Nan', although the family at first persisted in the fiction that she was his aunt. The boy was of course at first far too young to understand, and the situation was never referred to. But the child instinctively knew his true grandmother and refused all substitutes.

The family followed Chris's lead, and now everyone calls each other by their right names.

I began by talking about bonds with childminders. Perhaps the most intense non-family bond can be formed if the child has to go in hospital, especially if the child needs residential or long-term treatment. Quite rightly the importance of maintaining the mother-child bond in times of sickness is stressed, but we sometimes forget that the nurses, behind their professional exterior, do link in with a child's distress. They can and do come to love their charges, so much so that a child's death can be devastating for them. Their training and professionalism may prevent them from shedding public tears, and this can often be mistaken for callousness.

Louise worked for 38 years as an orthopaedic nurse at a children's residential hospital in the south of England. She never married, nor did she have children of her own. One of her charges was a little boy whom she nursed from his birth until he died in hospital at the age of twelve. In all that time the boy never walked or spoke. Louise grieved very strongly for him, for he had become almost like her own child. In the week after his death she had a most vivid dream of the boy in a beautiful garden. He was running towards her with open arms, something he had never been able to do in life. Louise later said the quality of the dream was like none she had never experienced before. In fact it didn't feel like a dream at all.

Some nurses do of course worry if they learn that a woman in labour seems to be communicating psychically with her baby during birth, but many not only know of this unspoken channel but use it in their work, especially with babies. If only more would feel able to admit it as did Kate, a former nurse living in Yorkshire, who told me of this other monitoring system that supplements and is sometimes faster than any technological checks. Kate was mentioned in Chapter 9 because since childhood she has had close psychic links with her mother, Jean.

'I accepted this sort of communication at home as we were very close,' she said, 'but I was surprised to find telepathy existed among the medical profession. Nurses on the Special Care Baby Unit would be sitting in the nurses' room having a cup of tea and suddenly disappear, then come back minutes later to say, "Oh, Jamie has just puked up and was going to inhale it." It was quite commonplace – they were so tuned in to the babies they just knew before any alarms that a certain baby would be about to stop breathing or was in trouble. I did it myself, both with children and adults. Suddenly I'd find myself half way down the ward without knowing why, and then see a patient who needed help breathing or whatever. It's all a question of fine tuning.'

Could it be the same qualities of mothering are those that make a good nurse: caring, vigilance and the little extra ingredient? Why are so many of the nurses who are especially 'in tune' with the patients reluctant to talk about this ability? Is it because the authorities would frown on relying on intuition? Yet if midwives and nurses could come up front more often, and say to mums,

'Yes, act on your instincts, we do it all the time and it works,' it would give mother-magic an official seal of approval and open the way to using intuition as one of the most valuable tools of mothering.

So what can we learn from the experiences of carers who have psychic links with children?

In Britain especially the barriers between children and adults who are not their parents can be great. Children are noisy, messy and time-consuming. They like being heard as well as seen, but in small doses are fun and can help to put life back into perspective. Perhaps we should remember that obnoxious children are like bad dogs: the fault of bad keepers. Let us remember also that often mothers don't have the time or energy to give their children the input and insight into a world outside the home which other adults can provide.

Children don't need expensive treats, just time and understanding. If your consciousness seems to have reached a plateau, try spending a few hours with children – they might open up psychic vistas you last saw when you knew Father Christmas was true and his grotto stretched all the way to fairyland, not just to the shoe department. At the very least, your input won't be wasted – after all, they are the generation who will be pushing our bath-chairs in years to come, so it's as well we get to know them.

13

Beyond the Grave

Dryring went to an island and married Barbaik, a pretty young girl. He lived with her for seven years and became the father of six children. But death passed through the country and Barbaik, his beautiful flower without blemish, perished.

Dryring went to another island and chose a new wife. After the marriage he moved her into his house. Sadly she was hard and cruel. She saw the bereaved children who looked at her and cried and roughly pushed them away.

She gave them neither beer nor bread and told them: 'You shall have hunger and cold.' She took away their blue cushions and told them: 'You shall sleep on the straw.' She took away their bright candles and told them: 'You shall stay in the darkness.' That evening the children cried. Lying on her bed, the cold ground, Barbaik heard them and resolved to return to them. She approached Our Father and said to him: 'Let me go to see my children.' And she continued to beg him until he gave permission for her to return to the Earth. But he told her that she must return before cock crow.

Barbaik raised her tired legs and crossed the walls of the cemetery. As she passed through the village the dogs drew back into their homes and the air shook with their howls. When she came to her house she found her eldest girl standing by the door.

'What are you doing there my dear daughter?' she asked her, 'and where are your brothers and sisters?' 'Why do you call me dear daughter?' replied the child. 'You are not my mother. My mother was beautiful and young, my mother had rosy cheeks. But you, you are pale as death.' 'How could I be beautiful and young? I come from the kingdom of the dead and so my face is white. How could I have rosy cheeks? I have been dead so long,' said Barbaik and went into her children's room where she found them crying.

She washed the first, she brushed the hair of the second, she consoled the third and the fourth, and she took the fifth in her arms as if to suckle her. Then she said to her eldest girl: 'Tell Dryring to come here.' When Dryring came, Barbaik cried with rage: 'I left beer and bread here and my children are hungry. I left them blue cushions and my children sleep on the straw. I left bright candles and my children sleep in the dark. If I have to return here again there will be trouble for you. Now the red cock crows and the gates of heaven are opening. Hark, the white cock crows and I can no longer stay.' Since that day, whenever Dryring and his wife heard the dogs bark they gave the children beer and bread and every time they heard the dogs howl they feared they might see the dead mother again.

This chilling Breton legend from *Le Foyer Breton* by Emile Souvestre (Nelson, 1910), like so many, mirrors real life. Mike, a down-to-earth builder living in the south of England, married Sally, a widow with three small boys. The youngest boy, John, was only two years old when Mike moved into their lives, and Mike found him naughty, defiant and hard to cope with.

'I often ended up losing my temper and smacking him,' Mike told me. 'I was always getting angry with him though I knew I shouldn't. I suppose I just wasn't used to living with kids, and he was so difficult to handle with his tantrums.'

One night a man appeared to Mike when he was by himself in the house. 'For Christ's sake, Mike,' said the man, 'don't smack the boy too hard. I know John's naughty but you're going to do something you'll regret if you don't stop it.' Then the figure disappeared. 'I'd never met John's dad but I recognized him straight away from a photo Sal had of him,' Mike said. 'I was terrified. From that time I never smacked the kid again. I've never told my wife about this. The lad is older now and we get on really well. But I tremble to think what might have happened if his dad hadn't come back to warn me.' Was it conscience that drove Mike to see the dead father? Was the apparition a projection from Mike's own mind which ordered him to change his attitude to the child? Or did the father's bond with his child allow him to come back, called by his child's distress to try to protect him? Once again, when exploring these matters I find that in the end the effect is more important than the cause. As a result Mike himself did become attached to the child.

Whatever our religious beliefs or lack of them, the severing of the mother-child bond by death is hard to come to terms with. As J.M. Barrie said in *The Little White Bird*: 'The only ghosts, I believe, who creep into this world, are dead young mothers returning to see how their children fare. There is no other inducement great enough to bring the dead back.' Dr Anthony Evans, who lives in Wiltshire, certainly believes this love carries on. He told me of the apparent return of his mother, who died when he was still quite young. He found her reappearance incredibly comforting as a child; it served to assure him that even though his mother could not be not with him physically, the bond between them could survive even death. Whether the mother does seem to survive death and can communicate with her children in a recognizable form or whether the bond remains less tangibly, in the form of the love created by the person in her lifetime, the experience can be enriching.

Anthony told me, 'In the last year of the Second World War I was living in a large family house in the Midlands with my father. My mother had died a month earlier after a long and painful illness. This particular night I lay awake, not thinking of my mother, when I was aware of two puffs of air on my face from above. The head of my bed pointed to the door, and in the past my mother had often looked in on her way to bed to check if I was awake. She did this by blowing on my face lightly. I would respond, if I was awake, with a "Goodnight, Mum," and so on.

'So I was really startled by this familiar happening. I sat up and looked around the darkened room. Then I got out of bed and went to my father's room across the landing. He was lying awake, in the dark, smoking his pipe. I told him what had happened. He thought a moment and said, "Obviously your mother looked in to see how you are – you know how she worries about you. Not scared, are you?" Denials from myself. Father said, "Get back to bed then, your mother won't want you wandering around at this hour." I went back to bed quite relaxed and quite sure that my mother had looked in on me.'

The response of Anthony's father helped to confirm the experience as a positive one for the boy. Too often the shocked replies of an adult when a child tells them he has seen his dead parent can make the child feel stupid, or worse still, wicked. Even if in scientific terms Anthony did not actually see 'a verifiable form of his mother' – whatever that might be – he was reassured that she was still there for him. What more important message can be given? For Anthony the truth of the incident was apparently confirmed when his own son appeared to know the grandmother who had died so long before he was even born.

'Thirty years after my mother died I was sitting with my young son looking through family photographs. To my surprise there was an old photograph of my mother, taken in 1941. I had only seen it a few times, a small fading photograph of a dark-haired woman of 45. My son had never seen it before. On an impulse I asked, "Who is this?" Quite casually my son said, "It's Gran." Thinking it a guess I pointed out, "But Gran (my wife's mother) has white hair and no glasses." My son looked at me as if I were slightly retarded. "It's my other Gran." I said, "Of course, of course," and left it there. My wife confirmed she had not shown him that photo nor any other ones of my mother previously, nor had anyone else. He recognized immediately, from among pictures of other middle-aged ladies, his grandmother, who had died long before he was born.'

The death of a child, especially in early childhood, is a prospect so awful that many of us find it hard even to think of. But some women who have lost children do believe that the bond between them and their beloved child goes on. It is very difficult for us to dispute their claims or to argue it is wish-fulfillment if we have not experienced this ourselves. Even they do not say it is possible, only that it happened.

Alison Athanassiou, who lives in Brisbane, Australia, lost her third child at birth but believes her infant not only comforted her but still comes to her husband, who has as yet not come to terms with the loss. She has had four children and has long experience of the night-waking and breast-feeding phenomena which we have discussed in earlier chapters. She has also had strong links with her children while they were in the womb.

She told me, 'Probably for me the most conclusive evidence of a link between the unborn baby and me was the absolute certainty of the sex of each child and the vivid dreams and visions of exactly how each would look, which were 100 per cent correct in every case.

'This was particularly valuable for me in the case of my third baby, Janet, who did not survive her birth. I was knocked out by general anaesthetic as the doctor tried to "save" her by ripping her out of me with forceps – even though everyone (except me) knew it was too late. As a result of the terrible injury to my cervix and perineum I spent two-and-a-half hours unconscious while being repaired and did not officially "know" that my baby had left her body. However, as soon as I woke and without anyone telling me, I knew she was dead. I remember looking round the recovery room to find her, as I felt she was waiting there for me. To this day I know she was there, looking down on her shocked and suffering mother with compassion, staying for half an hour or so until she was sure I had grasped the reality of the situation, and then leaving. I have never "felt" her again.

'I believe she has not been back in touch with me because I have largely come to terms with her loss and am back on track again (although one never gets over a baby's death). However the same cannot be said for Arthur, my husband. In the two years since her birth and death he has been a rock for me and my closest ally, but has not paid enough attention to his own grieving process. He is not particularly psychic nor is he as sure about eternal life or reincarnation as I am. Yet it is he who has been receiving messages from Janet. Nothing dramatic, but over the last two years whenever he has been feeling really bad and hopeless he feels a tug on his trouser leg or a touch on the lower back, exactly where a tiny child could reach. He has felt these touches a number of times, and we have interpreted them as Janet saying, "Pay attention, Dad. Learn what needs to be learned."

'He has never been frightened by this contact but happy and sad at the same time, and the touches are fewer and further apart nowadays. Perhaps he doesn't need to be reminded so often.

'I recalled while writing this that Janet actually waved goodbye to me in utero. The last movement before her heart faltered and I was put under was a rippling sort of salute which filled me with great sorrow, though I did not know why until much later.'

Jan Pattrick lives in Freshwater on the Isle of Wight. I first met Jan in the school playground while I was waiting for my children and she was waiting for her young daughter, Jade. Her four-year-old son Calum had died six months before, after only a few weeks at school. Next day in her comfortable family home Jan showed me pictures of Calum and told me his story, which began with one of those premonitions of doom that come from nowhere and which I have already discussed.

'Calum was a normal healthy four-year-old. A couple of months before last Christmas I first had the feeling something bad was going to happen. I phoned my mum. "Can we have a family Christmas?" I asked her. "I have this feeling we won't all be together again." "There isn't room for everyone here," Mum said. "Perhaps next year." But I knew that would be too late.'

The feeling returned to Jan in the most inappropriate surroundings. She and her husband Tony had taken the children to the White Mouse Inn in Chale, a fine old pub on the island with wonderful gardens for the children to play in and a beautiful view of the sea. The children were playing happily on the slides and swings in the garden, and all should have been well. But the feeling of danger lying in wait came to Jan more strongly than ever. 'I said to Tony, "I feel something dreadful is going to happen to us. We are too happy. We love each other, we've got three lovely children and enough money to scrape by and manage." We were never worried about material things so long as we could afford the odd trip out and a pub lunch sometimes. Tony said, "You musn't even think things like that."

'Not long afterwards Calum's tummy began to swell. He wasn't ill and I knew he wasn't overeating. He was starting school after Easter and I had bought him a school t-shirt a few weeks before. Now I just couldn't get it on him.

'Calum insisted his tummy didn't hurt. "There's nothing wrong with me, Mum," he said. But his stomach didn't go down. I knew something was dreadfully wrong. All the next day I put off contacting the doctor. At 5.30, just before it closed, I telephoned the surgery. "I haven't got an appointment," I told the receptionist, "but I need an opinion because my son's stomach is enlarged."

'When I showed the nurse at the Health Centre she fetched a doctor at once. The doctor prodded Calum's stomach and said he wasn't sure what it was. Calum lay on the bed and the nurse gave me some tea. The doctor sent us to Newport Hospital, where we stayed the night, and the doctors there gave Calum some blood tests and scans. They thought he had blocked lymph glands, and sent us to Southampton Hospital.

'I knew from the start Calum would die. My husband Tony went with him to Southampton and later phoned me from the ward to say the doctors had discovered a tumour.

'Calum became desperately ill that night and was rushed to Guy's Hospital in London; he was not expected to last the night. I went up by train. Calum was screaming when I got there, but he pulled through and the next morning was sitting up asking for chocolate yoghurt. The doctors said he would be all right but I said he was going to die. I realized I was upsetting Tony so in the end I kept quiet. Calum came home and went for treatment as an outpatient.

'One Wednesday he had been to chemotherapy as usual. Later in the day I phoned the hospital to say he was really ill and in pain, and the doctor said he would look at him in the morning. While Calum was having the treatment he had refused to go near anybody. He had lost his hair, had a massive plaster on his neck and his weight had dropped to 13 pounds. In the evening Calum was in the garden lying on the swinging hammock while I was pulling up the weeds when he suddenly said, "Come on Mum, it's the fashion show at school tonight." "How did you know it was on?" I asked, because I hadn't even bothered to mention it.

'He replied, "I just know." He was covered in mud and in so much pain, but I bundled him up and when we got there I sat him on my lap. He was dancing about, greeting everyone like his old self, and people were taking pictures of him. It was as if he was saying to everyone, "Here I am everybody. This is the last you'll see of me." "Hello, Mrs Pankhurst," he said to his teacher, as though he had just been off school with a cold. I couldn't believe the transformation in him. He hadn't been out for seven weeks. The next morning, he was brain-damaged and dying.

'I can't believe it was just a coincidence he suddenly wanted to go to the school. Two days previously Tony had been carrying him on his shoulders and we went for a walk past the church to the creek. Calum was holding his fishing rod. "When I die," he said suddenly, pointing to the churchyard, "I want to be buried there, not burned." "You aren't going to die," I told him.

'He had said nothing previously about dying, and he was apparently doing well on the treatment. "Promise me I can be buried there," he insisted.

'At 11 p.m. the night of the fashion show Calum started to be very sick. Eventually he was airlifted to Southampton but got there too late. He had a heart attack, followed shortly by another. The doctors said he would be all right but Calum was badly brain-damaged, blind and did not know us. We were given a choice: keep him alive with drugs or let him go with morphine. So that's what we did, let him go peacefully.

'Once the illness had started Calum had grown up so quickly it was unbelievable. I used to cuddle him and call him my little man. One day he said suddenly. "I'm not your little man any more, I'm your big man now." It was as if he was getting ready to die.

'Calum died at 2.10 in the morning on June 6th. Suddenly he clutched Tony's hand and looked at him. He couldn't see and we thought he didn't even know we were there. He couldn't even speak but he looked as if he could see something wonderful beyond Tony. "Look," said Tony, "he's all right."

Then Calum was gone. I felt as if Calum wanted to say something and show us what he could see.

'Calum was buried in the churchyard as he'd asked. After the funeral I went to bed, crying. In my sleep Calum came to me. "Mum, don't cry, I'm all right. I'm really happy now."

'I told only Tony and he was upset. Two weeks later Calum came to my sister-in-law in a dream and said, "Sarah, don't cry, I'm really happy." He loved his aunt very much. She later told me that two months before Calum became sick she'd dreamed of his funeral. She hadn't told me at the time because she hadn't wanted to frighten me.

'Though I held Calum in my arms when he was on morphine it really upset me that I never knew for sure whether he knew I was cuddling him. When Calum died I registered his death in Southampton and the body was brought back to the Isle of Wight. Pam, the lady at the funeral directors, had phoned me and said, "Come and see Calum. He looks lovely," but I hadn't wanted to know. I knew his spirit had gone.

'In the September after he died we were going away to Portugal for a holiday. The night before we left I had a dream in which I was registering Calum's death and Pam phoned me and asked me to go and see the body.

'This time I did, and when I looked at Calum his arm or leg

moved. But I went away and didn't tell anyone. Then I was at the funeral and I insisted the coffin be brought back up and opened. I could see people saying I was being a real prat, but I didn't care. Someone found a screwdriver and undid the lid and out jumped Calum and gave me a real cuddle. "Why are you burying me?" he asked, "I'm not dead."

'The dreams I had of Calum weren't like ordinary dreams. There was always a brilliant light round him. Calum comforted me and helped me to go on.

'While we were in Portugal Tony and I were sitting chatting, and Tony said I was looking much better. He asked if it was the holiday that had helped. I decided to try to tell him about the dream I'd had just before we came away. Before that dream I kept having flashbacks of the day of Calum's last week, the brain damage, bringing the body home, laying him out. I'd have a flashback in the middle of dinner and go upstairs so the other children wouldn't see me crying.

'Tony said when I told him about the dream, "I used to feel so helpless. When you got so upset in the day or at dinner, I used to go to Calum's bed and say, 'Calum, you've got to help your mum. I can't.' " It helped us both a lot, talking about it. It helped Tony especially to know that Calum had come to help me.

'Two weeks ago I had another dream in which Calum had cut the back of his legs really badly, gashed them open. I cuddled and cuddled him. In the dream I was so happy, and when I woke it wasn't like when you're a kid and dream of Christmas and then wake up disappointed when you realize it isn't after all. I didn't think, "Oh, it wasn't true," I felt better, really well inside, because I had seen him.

'While you're dreaming you want to open your eyes but you can't. Calum talks to me and I can see his face, surrounded by this massive light. It's so frustrating not being able to get there. Calum was always different from my other children. When he was about four I can remember him sitting between us in bed, one arm round me and one round his Dad. If we joked, "Whom do you love best?" he would always reply he loved us the same. Most kids of that age will go to whomever gives them the best deal at the time, but not Calum. He never played one off the other and never said anything, little though he was, to hurt anyone's feelings. I loved him so much. I used to look at him and think, "How could I cope if anything happened to you?" He didn't like playschool and just wouldn't settle, so I stopped sending him. It hurt me too much when he was unhappy. No one ever looked after Calum but me and his Dad from the day he was born till the day he died. It was different with the other children. They were more independent. Calum could not bear even a brief separation from me. I could never bear to be separated from him, either. I worked at the Red Lion pub in Freshwater some evenings to bring in a bit of extra money, and Calum would be waiting at midnight at the top of the stairs for me when I got home.

'You never think when you have children that they won't grow up. I felt I was better prepared than anyone else in the family because I had known Calum was going to die. Tony told me, "I feel sorry Calum doesn't come to me. But I hear things in my head and I wonder if they're true." I told him he must believe what he hears in his head. "You must listen to what your mind tells you." I am a totally different person from the one I was last year, before this happened. I believe this occurred for a purpose. I have become a "Leukaemia Buster", helping to raise money for other leukaemia sufferers and their families. I want to help other people now.

'I hope I keep having my dreams about Calum. It is not like having him here, of course; nothing can ease that pain. But at least I can see him and know he is happy.'

Jan believes that the bond between mother and child can go on after death. Even for those who cannot accept that a child can return physically to comfort his mother, few can deny that the love does not die with the child but lives on in what the child was and what the mother has become as a result of bearing that child. We cannot really believe otherwise, and we certainly cannot put it all down to wish-fulfilment or a psychological stage of the grieving process – unless we have been there.

Perhaps the strangest story I came across was that of Emily, who was widowed when her twin daughters Sarah and Louise were less than three. Each night the twins would kneel at their mother's feet, say their prayers, kiss their father's photograph and then jump into bed.

One night, when they were not much more than four years old, Sarah kept turning round and smiling during the prayers. Mum said, 'Come on, put your hands together like a good girl.' But Sarah continued to look over to the other side of the room. After prayers her mother said, 'Sarah, why did you keep turning round and smiling when we were saying our prayers?' 'I was smiling at Daddy,' she replied. 'But his photo's in the other room,' her mother said, puzzled.

'No, Mummy, Daddy was standing there on the other side of the room. I saw him.' Her mother told her off for making up stories and put the girls to bed.

Emily thought no more of the incident, but the next morning when she got up Sarah insisted, 'I did see Daddy standing on the other side of the room last night. He was really there.' Not long afterwards Sarah suddenly fell very ill and died. While she was ill her mother tried to persuade her to eat, but Sarah refused, saying, 'I don't want to eat. I want to go with my Daddy to heaven. He's all white and shiny.' Her mother replied, 'But what about us? If you went to heaven to be with Daddy we would miss you.' 'All right,' said Sarah, 'I'll ask if you and Louise can come too.' Soon after this incident, Sarah died.

Religion, science, philosophy have no real answers. But a mother's instincts can promise – not the return of the child – nothing can do that, and to the grieving parent that is the bitterest gall of all – but some assurance that the love of parent for child and child for parent is not of this lifetime only. Even the most sceptical can share in this feeling.

Christopher Booker, the *Sunday Telegraph* columnist, re-members: 'For as long as I can remember, every year on my birthday, which falls in October – my dear mother has recalled that, at the moment before I entered the world at 6.30 in the morning, she heard a blackbird singing in the garden outside. Every year for at least thirty years I have respectfully informed her that it could not have been a blackbird singing in October. It must have been a robin. Two weeks ago my mother died, and on Wednesday last, in a Dorset country churchyard, I had the sad task of placing her ashes in the earth. At that moment, a few yards from her grave, two birds began to sing very loudly. One was a robin, the other was a blackbird. I hope she was able to share the joke. Perhaps she arranged it.'

Was this another example of psychic communication, I asked him? He replied: 'Keenly aware though I am of "sixth sense" experiences and of the "hidden web" of significance surrounding our lives, and often involving nature, I cannot say that I had any special bond of this kind with my mother, although her mother was a very strong intuitive and had many extra-sensory experiences. I did have a teasing relationship with my mother, based on her rather dogmatic acceptance of what she was told (e.g. by weather forecasters in the media, which I would counter with intuitive common sense that weather forecasters were usually wrong, as a look out of the window might indicate!). The ongoing badinage about the blackbird was an example of this. My mother had established an *ideé fixe* which I knew to be wrong, but nothing could talk her out of it. That is why, as I lowered the ashes into the ground and heard both robin and blackbird striking up together, I had a smile on my face.'

14

Summing Up

Over the last thirteen chapters I have talked a lot about a mother's instincts but haven't said much about what all those magic vibes flying around do for women themselves. Most women, myself included, vowed before we became mothers that motherhood wouldn't change us one bit.

All those other mothers, harassed, disorganized, dragging along runny-nosed kids and weeping over Disney films while their children indifferently crunched popcorn and asked when the robots were coming – they simply hadn't got their act together. We were different, clearheaded, determined, efficient. Some women may indeed claim that motherhood really hasn't made one iota of difference to their existence, but I haven't met any of them. Those women are more likely to be flying over my head in the first-class compartment of Concorde than standing behind me in the supermarket queue or sitting next to me in the doctor's surgery with little Johnny's head jammed in a saucepan.

For many women, whether they do continue with careers or make motherhood their full-time job, motherhood changes not only their way of life but causes a deeper shift in the way they feel and are. But of course we weren't going to admit it could ever happen to us. So when the pregnancy hormones started flowing, we may have found ourselves sniffling a bit at the old *Lassie* films – but we reassured ourselves that it was a temporary physiological hiccup.

Come the first couple of years or so of babyhood and we were organizing the funeral of a squashed hedgehog with berries for his journey to heaven (just to please the kids, of course). That was just the effect of the hormone prolactin, oozing from every pore, we assured ourselves, as we blotted milk from the front of our jumpers and the tears from our eyes with amazing regularity.

Ten years later you're a lady executive late for an important meeting. You see some kid (not even yours) crying by the roadside because he's lost his dinner money and has missed the school bus and what do you do? Drive by? What if it had been your kid and all those other mothers had just driven by?

So what didn't you know in those glorious but strangely empty pre-baby days? For a start you could not comprehend the inherent instincts that link you forever not only to your own very special (and the best ever created) infant but to every lame duckling that quacks at your door. Nor is the effect confined to the first nine months or even nine years. It is a magic that once it touches your life may knock your rose-tinted spectacles for six but shows you a technicolour world you only glimpsed as a child.

An Abyssinian noblewoman explained this far better than I can: 'As a mother a woman is another person than the woman without child. She carries the fruit of the night for nine months in her body. Something grows into her life that never again departs from it. She is a mother and remains a mother even though her child dies. Though all her children die. For at one time she carried the child under her heart and it does not go out of her heart ever again.'[1]

Abyssinian noblewomen may react like that, but surely today's mothers are a tougher breed? Not so for many women, who find a constant conflict between the call of the child and the single-mindedness necessary to compete and succeed. Not so, according to Julie Loyd of Walden Island, the most northerly island off the west coast of the United States. Julie enjoys a psychic bond with her children as well as a simple lifestyle: no electricity but seals on the rocks and goats in the garden. Julie says she came from a straight-laced Calvinist upbringing which stressed hard work, sobriety and not showing emotions, and

[1] Quoted by Leo Frobenius in *Der Kopf als Schickeal* (Munich, 1924).

describes herself as 'very left-brain' (the left-hand side of the brain controls functions such as language, writing and mathematics – which Julie concentrated on at college and did well at. The right-hand side is reckoned to control perception, fantasy, art and music appreciation and – some researchers believe – may even control the psychic functions). Julie says she always had 'real trouble with emotional people. Yet now I find myself weeping over babies I don't know.'

So what knocked out the left-brain superiority? 'This tenderness certainly wasn't there before I had kids. I'd never felt any sympathy towards babies unless they were both quiet and cute. Now I can hardly bear to hear of babies who need help. I'm planning a trip to Germany to visit my mother's aunts, and can hardly stand the thought of not nipping over to Romania and collecting a few little ones from the orphanages.'

Just words? One American woman saw a video of the Romanian orphans and was struck by one particular child. She dreamed she found him, and armed with only his photo (taken of the telly while he was on it) she went to Romania and found the child in the place she had seen in her dreams.

It isn't just an emotional change that motherhood wreaks. Women who have never had a psychic experience in their lives, or certainly not since they were children, suddenly start seeing things and knowing things other people don't. Julie told me: 'I find that my psychic experiences are getting fairly frequent – I always figured I was immune to psychic phenomena but in the years since the birth of my children I've come almost to rely on fortunate coincidences and serendipity. Do you suppose it is the children or meditation or what?'

I should think it is a combination of all three. Quite a few women on becoming mothers do find that they start seeing ghosts or knowing in advance what is going to happen, with amazing regularity. Even those women who were psychically and spiritually orientated before having children find that motherhood radically changes the nature of their peak experiences. As a mother you can't get away from kids in the psychic world, even if they're not your own (any more than you could leave the kid who'd lost his bus fare and dinner money standing by the roadside).

Maria Campbell of Victoria, Australia, has had premonitions since childhood. We have already heard how she told her mum that grandad had died minutes before a relative arrived at the door with the news. Maria's psychic experiences continued into her adult life, and she often had dreams of disasters that she would hear confirmed next day on the news. Since becoming a mother, however, it is danger to children that fills Maria's precognitive dreams, not only her own (remember it was she who knew that her eight-month-old son Alex was about to swallow a fistful of needles and was able to avert this potential disaster, as we saw in Chapter 2) but children she doesn't even know.

'I sometimes get images of houses burning and children trapped,' she told me. 'Sure enough next day it will be on the news. It usually starts off with me thinking "What would I do if my house caught fire? My babies – how could I get them out?" And then it will go on, the smoke and the flames, all so real it's scary, and then I'll find out it's happened to another family I didn't even know. Lately it has been children in my visions. I home in on the feelings of the child as she or he is calling out. I feel it and pick it up like a radio transmitter.'

But then being a mother does change everything. The psychic kick-start can even be activated before the child is born. Elspeth, a solicitor living on the south coast of England, said that while she was in labour with her son 20 years ago a beautiful, tiny, grey-haired nurse in a grey dress and no apron kept popping in and out of the hospital ward to see her. 'She was lovely, chatting to me and holding my hand. She had a beautiful circular brooch with brilliant pearls, emeralds, diamonds and rubies. I remember thinking she was the only one in the room wearing jewellery apart from the other nurses' clip-on watches. She held my hand

and talked. She told me I was having a boy. All the way through she kept encouraging me. It was wonderful.

'The doctor at last told me I had had a little boy, which I knew anyway because the old nurse had told me. I had a sleep and woke up starving, demanding my breakfast. They told me it was dinner time. I asked if I could talk to the older lady nurse with the beautiful brooch; I wanted to thank her for being so kind to me. But nobody knew her. I said, "But she was there," and they started talking about childbed fever and seeing a psychiatrist. So I shut up straight away and never said another word about her till I got home. But I was very puzzled. I told my dad and he asked me for details of her. "You daft hap'orth," he told me, "it was your grandma come to see you were all right." Then he remembered I had only been 18 months old when she had died, so it wasn't surprising I hadn't recognized her. He took a picture out of his wallet, one I had never seen before. It was his mum, and there she was, the kindly older nurse, wearing the brooch. I can picture her now – she wasn't insubstantial. She looked as real as you or I, and she held my hand all the way through labour. I told Mum and she said, "Oh, Dad's filling you with his weird ideas again." But I knew better.'

Elspeth was nearly carted off to a psychiatrist before she realized her 'ministering angel' was just that and kept quiet to the professionals. Professionals, as we have seen, can get very worried about these things (unless you are lucky enough to get a psychic midwife like the ones we met in Chapter 6).

Seeing such ghosts could be put down to 'the peculiarities of birth' as one obstetrician, more interested in the physical than psychic framework, suggested to me. But mothers may go on seeing or feeling presences no one else can see long after their child's birth. And even those women who once ate quantum physicists for dinner will find they have a pretty hard job proving their case. Of course husbands can be the most sceptical (though in Chapter 10 we met some who came out with one or two strange tales). Many a man will just smile and mutter 'hormones' when his partner tries to explain she has just seen a ghost. Sonia, however, was able to give her husband a bit of a surprise when he said the ghost in the baby's bedroom was all in her mind.

'My husband, baby daughter and myself moved into an old weaver's cottage which was about 150 years old. From the first I felt a very strong presence there, especially in my baby daughter's room. The room she slept in was a back bedroom overlooking fields; it looked out on a very pretty view. When I went into her room, I often smelled pipe tobacco as though an old man was in there. I felt as though he was sitting in a rocking chair looking out of the window. My husband just laughed and wouldn't take me seriously. But two years later he was modernizing the cellar and helping to take out an old fire range when underneath he found a white clay churchwarden's pipe in perfect condition.'

Some years later Sonia had another psychic experience connected with her daughter. 'It was early morning. I was in bed when the cat wanted to go out, so I went downstairs – it was about 6.45. I went back to bed but I knew it would soon be time to get my daughter up for school. We were sharing a bedroom then.

'Suddenly a figure appeared at the bottom of my daughter's bed. I was puzzled; I thought at first that someone had broken into the house.

'Then a strange humming noise came from the vision. When I looked I saw clearly a lady dressed in white, wearing not western clothes but what looked like a sari with a sort of veil across it. The face appeared dark, but I could not make out the features. The white material sparkled as though there were sequins or silver thread sewn into it. She stood at the foot of my daughter's bed for several minutes, and seemed to be looking at her, not at me. Then she turned and walked out of the open door.'

According to some researchers I shouldn't have been able to bond with my own son Jack at all. His was the most difficult and painful birth, and I was very ill afterwards. I bottle-fed Jack, too, and he slept in another room, so there shouldn't have been a chance of so much as a whiff of the paranormal. But from the first my relationship with him was pure magic. As I said earlier, I think once I was no longer trying to be Super Mum, or to prove to the world that motherhood hadn't changed me one bit, my instincts were given free rein.

When Jack was six weeks old the family went on holiday to Brittany. It was a hot afternoon, towards the end of July in 1984, and we were visiting Suscinio, a ruined chateau near the market town of Sarzeau. John had taken the older children, Tom and Jade, exploring, so I sat feeding Jack on what would have been a window seat but was now just rough stone, in one of the old round towers. There was nothing in the room but the remains of an old fireplace. As I glanced up I became aware that there was a fire burning in an iron grate, and a woman dressed in long robes sitting in a high wooden chair next to the fire feeding her baby. She was looking at me and I looked back. We just sat there feeding our babies. I was not frightened nor even disturbed, because it seemed the most natural thing, just two mothers and their babies. I felt that even if I got up I could not reach her, as if there was some barrier I could not see. As I heard Tom and Jade calling there was a sudden rush of wind and the fire went out. The lady got up and walked through the door, trailing her robes and carrying the baby, as my husband John came in. He saw nothing. He tells me I said, 'It was because we were both mothers that I saw her.' Certainly, we were linked somehow through our babies. It was a deeply satisfying experience. However, the next year when we went back to Brittany and went to Suscinio on a misty day in October, I did not feel that I could go inside.

I saw the phantom (or product of the heat, according to my husband) once more on that first holiday, walking with the baby on her hip down a path near the chateau moving towards a deserted cove. I knew she was taking the baby to Britain because it wasn't safe for them to stay in the chateau. To this day I don't know whether it was the heat, my imagination or whether the phantom and I walked together a short way because being mothers was temporarily a stronger link than the boundaries of time.

We have already seen that some women feel that it was a dead relative who somehow alerted them to an infant's distress. Peg not only saw her mother but heard and felt her. The only thing Peg couldn't understand was what her mum was doing in the house in the middle of the night.

Peg woke up suddenly to find her mother shaking her awake and telling her 'Wake up quickly, it's the baby. He needs help, urgently.'

Still half-asleep Peg jumped up, wondering why her mother hadn't gone to the baby herself, and rushed to his room. The infant's face was face turning blue. Another minute and he would have choked. She managed to resuscitate the baby, but when he was checked no medical reason could be found for the attack.

Much, much later Peg sank back exhausted into bed, glad that her little one was safe. Only then did the strangeness of the experience strike her. Her mother had been dead for three years, and had never even seen the child.

What then is magic, what natural?

From where comes the superhuman strength that makes a five-foot, eight-stone mother lift heavy garage doors off her child or find the courage to leap on the bonnet of a moving car to stop it running into her children? In the animal kingdom the ferocity of the mother in defence of her young is well documented, but for the human mother there is the fleeting moment when she must consciously decide 'my life for the child's', and can only trust she finds the strength to save him. One story, that of Julie Henderson of Yorkshire, struck a special chord in my heart, not only because of her incredible strength and courage but because it is a real-life situation with no instant happy ending. Her instincts paid off but the price was very high. Julie not only went through terrible physical suffering after saving her 14-month-old son Reece from being crushed by the wheels of a juggernaut lorry, but was temporarily rejected by the very child she almost died to save.

Julie's skirt had got caught under the wheel of a juggernaut as it suddenly pulled away from the kerb. Reece would also have been crushed had Julie not held the pushchair away from the wheels as she was being dragged along. Throughout the agony her thoughts were for Reece, and her first question as she was dragged crushed and semi-conscious from beneath the lorry was 'Is Reece all right?' She told me: 'All I felt was that I wanted to get Reece out of the way of the lorry. I suppose I did have a special strength that day. I wasn't bothered about myself. All I thought was I'd got to save him, and even afterwards through all the pain all I thought about was my baby. I do think mums have this special power in times of danger. The power of the maternal instinct is incredibly strong.'

It was not until she was at the hospital and had been shown her son well and unscratched that she could allow herself to face her own dreadful injuries and the fear that she might lose her leg. It took five months of painful treatment to save the limb, but, she told me, it was worth it. 'Reece was a very special baby, my first child and very much wanted. It must have been that. I just couldn't have lost him. It's surprising what you can do if your child's life is threatened. If it's your child, I don't know what it is but something comes out of you and you just do what you have to do. To save my son from what I've been through, I'd do it again tomorrow.'

But as I said, there was no instant happy ending. Reece had been frightened at the sight of his mother swathed in bandages while she was in hospital, and his last memories of her were of the day of the accident, marred by blood, noise and her apparent desertion of him. He was too young to understand his mother's sacrifice.

Julie's mother looked after him while she was in hospital, and when Julie hobbled back through the front door for what she hoped was to be the happy reunion Reece clung, screaming, to his grandmother. Julie didn't give up, though it wasn't till some weeks later after endless tantrums and tears that Reece climbed onto her lap and cuddled her for the first time since the accident.

Julie's story echoes what I have been saying throughout the book. Yes, there is magic – and sometimes it's all we have to keep us going – but there are no promises of an easy ride.

The magical bond of motherhood calls into question many of the assumptions of the material world. We have seen that the maternal link is no guarantee of happiness, but we are nevertheless joined from the day we first recognize we carry a new life within us till the tiny bundle is 30, six foot and on the other side of the world, and forever afterwards. Although even from the beginning of an infant's life we should not attempt to own his or her soul, at the deepest level our offspring carry our love and can call on us by tugging on this unbreakable, invisible cord.

We may all in some way and to some degree feel the bond of motherhood. For many of us it will touch our everyday worlds rather than being manifest in life-and-death situations. We should follow our instincts; if an infant knows his cry is heard and answered, then he will naturally take over his own psyche and life, secure that we are there if he needs us. It is the children whose call, whether psychic or physical, goes unheeded who need to stay close and stifle us with their fears.

However you interpret the call – you may hear a voice or just have a feeling deep down in your gut – go along with it. What have you to lose compared with what you have to gain? Remember that many of the practice panics that don't come immediately true may be a kind of psychic rehearsal, to prepare us so we know what to do when the real crisis hits.

We can use our 'mind-hopping' ability to help our children in difficult times, by picking up their sadness or uncertainty even when they have said nothing. As our children come into contact with an exciting but sometimes hostile world our unspoken sympathy and kind gestures can help them to feel accepted and valued. We can't fight their schoolyard battles for them but we can send our psychic armies out to help.

When our children reach adolescence it is sometimes this unspoken bond that can alert us to trouble when actual communication is at a minimum. We can help our children go into adulthood secure in the knowledge there is a deep love between us, a psychic safety net.

This may make mothers sound like little Mother Courages, always smiling, never screaming or saying all those things psychologists tell us will damage our offspring for life. Of course we all do blow our tops on occasion, but that is where the underlying psychic link can carry us through, not only in major crises but in the everyday hassles that make up 99 per cent of family life.

The psychic bond can also alert you to your child's health and well-being. Mothers' instincts are often not taken seriously by health professionals, and women can be over-awed by modern technology and its seeming expertise. Yet from the first mothers can know things, even about their unborn babies, that the machines and experts don't necessarily pick up.

Supplement medical advice where necessary with your own intuitions. In a situation where there is no clear-cut answer, follow your instincts, and if in doubt, insist on a second opinion. As well as a warning of problems the bond can be a reassurance that all will be well.

You are part of your child and your child is a part of you, so don't be afraid to voice your intuitions any more than you would be afraid to pick up on your own body's signals. This link continues even as you grow physically apart. You know your child's patterns and needs better than anyone else, and so you can help the medical and education professionals help your child in the best way possible.

As I have said, I do not believe that there are any ways to increase or harness these instincts, though I accept that some people will find that techniques such as visualization or meditation help keep them in touch with their spirituality. But even if you feel ready to scream and drown your child in the magical waterfall you're visualizing, don't worry. Many of the most magical birth experiences happened to those women whose strength had run out. Of course you should aim for the gentlest, most spiritual birth, if that is what you feel is right for you and your infant, but don't worry if you don't fall instantly in love with him or her. The maternal physical, emotional and psychic bond is a cord that can't be cut; it will be there tomorrow and for the rest of your lives.

In the modern consumer world we are told that if we buy a certain product or sign ourselves and our families up for special courses (none of them free) we can increase our happiness, success or progress towards inner understanding. But a mother's instincts do come free (if you don't count the inbuilt clause about blood, sweat and tears as well as all those golden smiles and special moments). I'm not about to get rich quickly by asking you to send me a thousand pounds in return for some 'instinct potion'. For you've already got the elixir, though perhaps you don't yet recognize or trust it yet.

The magic link is there for us all if we just stop worrying about whether our three-year-old is socially adjusted when he bops someone at playschool. The magic lies in quietude, not constant activity, and in accepting what we and our children are, not what we would like ourselves/them to be. It is not to be found in material goodies but in those moments when you and your child come into contact with the natural world that was there before the theme parks – the woods, the shores, the urban open spaces where you can just be together. Time is limited for us all, so leave the housework, the clubs and organized sports. Make a place and time for yourself and your child every day – even ten unbroken minutes will do. Turn off the phone, tape up the door bell for this 'quiet time'. The world will come back if it's got something urgent to say. The days of childhood are fleeting and precious – ask any woman who has lost a child.

Mother-magic is not an unattainable dream. This book is not just a collection of amazing stories about other people. Their stories are or could be yours. The message is there in every experience – just open your heart, love and accept yourself and your child. Within ourselves lies all we need to care for our young. In motherhood we lose the sense of being alone and separate from others, physically, emotionally and psychically. It may get a bit crowded at times in the womb and in our beds as the toddler barges his way in for the third time in an hour. But the love and trust of our children is the most precious gift of all, and our path to immortality.

Helpful Addresses

I am always pleased to hear from readers, and can be contacted through my publishers. Parents may also find the following addresses useful at times of crisis – psychic or otherwise.

BRITAIN

Alternative Therapies

British Homoeopathic Association
27a Devonshire Street
London W1N 1RJ

Tel: 071–935 2163

Medically-qualified doctors who practise homoeopathy.

Homoeopathic Development Foundation
19a Cavendish Square
London W1M 9AD

Tel: 071–629 3205

The National Federation of Spiritual Healers
Old Manor Farm Studio
Church Street
Sunbury-on-Thames
Middlesex TW16 6RG

Tel: 0932 783164

National Institute of Medical Herbalists
34 Cambridge Road
London SW7

Tel: 071–228 4417

Send a SAE for a register of practitioners.

Rebirthing
Liz Cornish, Registered Rebirther
Flat B
2 Wandsworth Common West Side
London SW18 2EL

Tel: 081–870 9284

Antenatal Support

Foresight
Old Vicarage
Church Lane
Witley
Godalming
Surrey GU8 5PN

Tel: 042879 4500

For help and information on pre-conceptual care.

Bereavement

Compassionate Friends
Mrs Gill Hoder, National Secretary
6 Denmark Street
Clifton
Bristol BS1 5DQ

Tel: 0272 292778

International organization for bereaved parents.

Miscarriage Association
18 Stoneybrook Close
West Bretton
Wakefield
West Yorks WF4 4TP

Tel: 0924 85515

SANDS (Stillbirth and Neonatal Death Society)
28 Portland Place
London W1N 4DE

Tel: 071–436 5881

Support after Termination for Abnormality (SATFA)
22 Upper Woburn Place
London WC1H 0CP

Tel: 071–387 7041

Breast-feeding

Association for Breast-feeding Mothers
18 Lucas Court
Winchfield Road
London SE26 4TJ

Tel: 081–778 4769

Support from other women who have breast-fed.

La Leche League of Great Britain
BM3424
London WC1N 3XX

Tel: 071–242 1278 or 071–404 5011

Details of the La Leche group and leader nearest you; breast-feeding
and maternal support groups. Source of excellent reading material.

Counselling

Parentline
Rayfa House
57 Hart Road
Thunderseley
Essex SS7 3PD

Tel: 0268 757077

Organization for parents under stress.

Parents Anonymous
8 Manor Gardens
Islington
London N7 6LA

Helpline: 071–263 8918

For any parents afraid they may abuse their child.

The Tavistock Clinic
Tavistock Centre
120 Belsize Lane
London NW3 5BA

Tel: 071–435 7111

Child and family therapy and psychotherapy.

Crying Babies

CRY-SIS
BM Box Cry-sis
London WC1N 3XX

Tel: 071–404 5011

Help for parents with crying babies.

Labour and Childbirth

Active Birth Centre
55 Dartmouth Park Road
London NW5 1SL

Tel: 071–267 3006

For information and courses on all aspects of pregnancy, birth and breast-feeding, and the hire or sale of Aqua Birth Pools. *Water Birth* by Janet Balaskas and Yehudi Gordon, which offers comprehensive advice on the use of water throughout pregnancy, birth and infancy, is available from the Centre.

Association of Radical Midwives
62 Greetby Hill
Ormskirk
Lancs L39 2DT

Tel: 0695 72776 or 081–580 2991

British Acupuncture Association and Register
34 Alderney Street
London SW1V 4EU

Tel: 071–834 1012

For alternative pain relief in labour. Promotes alternatives for a more meaningful childbirth experience, non-violent birth for mother and child, breast-feeding and family togetherness and infant bonding.

The Garden Hospital
Sunny Gardens Road
Hendon
London NW4

Tel: 081–203 0111

The Garden Hospital is a private hospital that supports active childbirth and that aims to provide a supportive and informative environment for parents and baby during pregnancy and continuing well into the first three months. Attention to breathing based on yoga techniques has replaced other techniques in the preparation for birth. Regular antenatal days bring together expectant and new mothers, obstetricians, midwives, yoga and baby massage teachers, plus guest lecturers on subjects such as homoeopathy and cranial osteopathy and the spiritual and psychic aspects of birth, as well as issues relating to pregnancy, birth and life.

Maternity Alliance
15 Britannia Street
London W1X 9JP
Tel: 071–837 1265
Have produced a birth-plan form.

Premature Babies
Nippers
The Sam Segal Perinatal Unit
St Mary's Hospital
Praed Street
Paddington
London W2
Tel: 071–725 1487

Single Parents
Gingerbread
35 Wellington Street
London WC2E 7BN
Tel: 071–240 0953
Groups plus practical help and advice.

Spiritual and Psychic Experiences
Alister Hardy Research Centre for Religious and Spiritual Experience
The Reverend George Wakefield, Director
Westminster College
Oxford OX2 9AT
Tel: 0865 243006

IANDS (UK) – International Association for Near-death Studies
David Lorimer, Director
The Old School House
Hampnett
Northleach
Glos GL54 3NN
Tel: 0451 60869

Support

Hyperactive Children's Support Group
71 Whyke Lane
Chichester
West Sussex PO19 2LD
Tel: 0903 725182

Meet-A-Mum Association (MAMA)
3 Woodside Avenue
London SE25 5DW
Tel: 081–654 3137

Contact them for the group nearest you.

National Childbirth Trust
Alexandra House
Oldham Terrace
Acton
London W3 6NH
Tel: 081–992 8637

For ante- and postnatal support, toddler and baby groups, Caesarean
and postnatal depression support.

National Step-family Association
162 Tennyson Road
Cambridge CB1 2DP

National Women's Register
245 Warwick Road
Solihull
West Midlands B92 7AH
Tel: 021–706 1101

Lively groups of women of all ages, who prove that there *is* life after
childbirth.

Parents for Safe Food
Britannia House
1–11 Glenthome Road
London W6 0LF

Tel: 081–748 9898

Pre-school Playgroups Association
61–63 Kings Cross Road
London WC1X 9LL

Tel: 071–833 0991

For information on playgroups for the under-fives in Great Britain.

Twins and Multiple Births Association
20 Redcar Close
Lillington
Leamington Spa
Warwicks CV32 7SU

Tel: 0926 22688

Women's Health Network
57 Chalton Street
London NW1 1HU

Tel: 071–383 3841

Working Mothers Association
77 Holloway Road
London N7 8JZ

Tel: 071–700 5771

For practical help and information.

UNITED STATES

Adoption

AASK (Aid to Adoption of Special Kids)
657 Mission Street
Suite 601
San Francisco,
CA 94105

Tel: (800) 23A–ASK1 (for information on adoption or sponsorship)

Assistance and support in the adoption of children with special needs.

Bereavement

The Compassionate Friends
P.O. Box 1347
Oakbrook,
IL 60521
Tel: (313) 323–5010

SIDS (Sudden Infant Death Syndrome)
Clearing House
1555 Wilson Boulevard
Suite 600
Rosslyn,
VA 22209
Tel: (703) 552–0870

Breast-feeding

The Human Lactation Centre
Dana Raphael, Director
666 Sturges Highway
Westport,
CT 06880
Tel: (203) 259–5995

La Leche League
9616 Minneapolis Avenue
P.O. Box 1209
Franklin Park,
IL 60131–820
Tel: (312) 455–7730
Breast-feeding support and literature

Labour and Childbirth

The Childbirth Education Foundation
James E. Peron, Director
P.O. Box 5
Richboro,
PA 18954
Tel: (215) 357–2792

Informed Homebirth, Informed Birth and Parenting
P.O. Box 3675
Ann Arbor,
MI 48106

Tel: (313) 622–6857 (please phone between 9 a.m. and 5 p.m. EST)

For expectant and new parents, providing information on alternatives for safe childbirth, parenting and education.

Waterbirths (US and International)
Karil Daniels
Point of View Productions
2477 Folsom Street
San Francisco,
CA 94110

Tel: (415) 931–0948

For the video *Water Baby: Experiences of Water Birth*, filmed in France, the USA and the USSR; *Waterbirth Resources List*, an extensive listing of experienced waterbirth practitioners in the USA and internationally, and *The Water Baby Information Book* and other waterbirth resources.

Support

National Organization of Mothers of Twins Clubs Inc.
12404 Princess Jeanne N.E.
Albuquerque,
NM 87112–4640

Tel: (505) 275–0955

CANADA

Bereavement

Canadian Foundation for the Study of Infant Deaths
4 Lawton Boulevard
Toronto
Ontario M4B 1V2

Tel: (416) 967–1314

Support

Aid for New Mothers
994 Bathurst Street
Toronto
Ontario M5R 3G7

Tel: (416) 535-2368

Family Service Bureau
1801 Toronto Street
Regina
Saskatchewan S4P 1M7
Tel: (306) 757-6675

AUSTRALIA

Alternative Therapies
The Childbirth Education Association of Australia (NSW)
127 Forest Road
Hurstville
NSW 2220
Tel: 02-574-927

Breast-feeding
Nursing Mother's Association of Australia

5 Glendale Street,
Nunawading
Victoria 3131

Tel: 03-877-5011

16 Johanssen Street,
Alice Springs
NT 5750

2 Queen's Road
Asquith
NSW 2078

Ross Street
Northgate
Queensland 4013

Support
Family Support Cottage
23 Victor Road
Brookvale
NSW 2100

Tel: 02-93-5600

Women's Community Health Centre
6 Mary Street
Hindmarsh
SA 5006

Tel: 08-46-6521